THE **Nova S** BUCKET LIST

25 UNFORGETTABLE EXPERIENCES, ADVENTURES AND DESTINATIONS, SELECTED BY NOVA SCOTIA'S BEST TRAVEL WRITERS

Dale Dunlop and Alison Scott

FORMAC PUBLISHING COMPANY LIMITED
HALIFAX

Formac Publishing Company Limited recognizes the support of the Province of Nova Scotia through Film and Creative Industries Nova Scotia. We are pleased to work in partnership with the Province of Nova Scotia to develop and promote our creative industries for the benefit of all Nova Scotians. We acknowledge the support of the Canada Council for the Arts which last year invested $157 million to bring the arts to Canadians throughout the country.

Canada Council   Conseil des arts
for the Arts   du Canada

Cover design: Gwen North
Cover images: (clockwise from top) Nova Scotia River Runners, Dale Dunlop, Dennis Jarvis/Flickr, Shutterstock

Library and Archives Canada Cataloguing in Publication

Title: The Nova Scotia bucket list: 25 unforgettable experiences, adventures and destinations selected by Nova Scotia's best travel writers / Dale Dunlop & Alison Scott.
Names: Dunlop, Dale, 1951- author. | Scott, Alison, 1954- author.
Description: Includes index.
Identifiers: Canadiana 20200213466 | ISBN 9781459506336 (softcover)
Subjects: LCSH: Nova Scotia—Guidebooks. | LCSH: Nova Scotia—Description and travel. | LCGFT: Guidebooks.
Classification: LCC FC2307 .D86 2020 | DDC 917.1604/5—dc23

Formac Publishing Company Limited
5502 Atlantic Street
Halifax, Nova Scotia, Canada
B3H 1G4
www.formac.ca
Printed and bound in Canada.

PHOTO CREDITS: 123RF: 79; Bigstock: 14, 17, 57, 106, 122; Black Loyalist Heritage Centre: 71; Cabot Links: 137; Canadian Museum of Immigration at Pier 21: 11, 12, 13; Cape Breton Highlands National Park: 141; Cobequid Eco Trails Society: 127, 133; David Baillieul: 26, 27, 28, 29; Dennis Jarvis/Flickr: 4, 19, 22 (bottom), 44, 83, 89–91, 93, 95, 119 (top); Donna Barnett: 33; Highland Links: 136; Ian Preston/Flickr: 147 (bottom); iStock: 18, 23, 40 (top), 86 (top), 87, 101, 107, 109, 116, 117, 125, 130, 135, 141, 142 (top); Jamie Robertson/Domaine de Grand Pré: 108; Kelly Mercer/Flickr: 21; Larry/Flickr: 123 (bottom); Nova Scotia River Runners: 110, 114, 115; Parks Canada/Chris Green: 56, 58; Peter Zwicker/Bacalao Photo: 53, 54, 55; Piqsels: 126; Pixabay: 63, 85, 132, 142 (bottom); PxHere: 144, 148; Sarah J./Flickr: 80; Shawn Kent/Flickr: 111 (top), 112; Shubenacadie River Adventure Tours: 117; Shutterstock: 10 (top), 16, 24, 31 (bottom), 40 (bottom), 41, 65, 82, 84, 96, 102, 134, 140, 143, 146, 147 (top); Stan Shebs: 86 (bottom); Stella van der Lugt: 152, 153; Triton Alliance: 42; Trout Point Lodge: 59, 60, 61; Zoe Lucas: 154; 156 (top); 158; all other photos by Dale Dunlop.

To our parents, who inspired in us a love of this wonderful province called Nova Scotia.

CONTENTS

INTRODUCTION

I'm writing this introduction while self-isolating at our home in St. Margaret's Bay due to the COVID-19 pandemic that has stricken the world in 2020 and virtually shut down Nova Scotia. The idea of being able to get out and travel throughout the province seems absurd from my perspective today. But it won't always be that way. The pandemic will pass and by the time you are reading this people will be more anxious than ever to get outdoors and explore. However, it may be years before most people get over their fears of air travel, with crowded airports and even more crowded airplanes. In the case of cruise ships, it may never happen. That is why I believe a book like this, which is aimed primarily at my fellow Nova Scotians but also for those travelling to our beautiful province, is timelier than ever.

My first foray into commercial writing was in 1995 when Formac published *Exploring Nova Scotia*, which was meant to be the most comprehensive travel book ever written about my native province. It followed years of travelling by car, on foot, on cross-country skis and by canoe and kayak over every inch of Nova Scotia that I possibly could traverse. It also involved visiting hundreds of attractions — from museums and art galleries to national, provincial and municipal parks to ceilidhs, concerts and tattoos. One of the most enjoyable parts of researching that book was eating at a wide range of restaurants, from chip wagons and fried fish trucks to some of the finest dining establishments in Canada. Part of the experience was staying in as many of Nova Scotia's country inns as possible, and I discovered that we have a lot of them.

All this was done at my own expense, which fortunately my day job as a litigation lawyer permitted me to do. It was important that the book be an accurate and unbiased account of every place and experience that went into it. My approach was to only include what I thought would be worthwhile for someone visiting the province for the first time or someone who had lived here their entire life. If an experience wasn't up to snuff, it didn't get into *Exploring Nova Scotia*.

To my pleasant surprise, the book was well received and sold well. So well that Formac asked me to do a revised edition. This time I enlisted the assistance of my wife, Alison Scott, who had been with me on almost all the adventures described in the first edition. Once again, we set out to find as many new places and experiences as we could and to revisit many other ones. When we tabulated the number of entries for this revised edition, published in 1998, it came to an astonishing 445. We followed with revised versions every few years until 2010. Alison and I had produced a series of Canadian best sellers about the province we love and hopefully in the process introduced thousands of people to new experiences and a better appreciation of all that Nova Scotia has to offer.

The internet has substantially changed the way people get their information, especially about travel. While guidebooks still have their place, they are almost out of date from the moment they are published. However, there is still a market for specialty travel books that feature places and experiences you cannot easily find online. So it was with the next book I worked on: *25 Outdoor Adventures in Halifax*, written with fellow adventurer Ryan Barry, owner of Great Earth Expeditions, and published in 2016. Between us we paddled, hiked, snowshoed, cross-country skiied, snorkeled and biked our way through many places close to Halifax that had never been written about before.

This new collection of 25 unforgettable experiences and adventures is a combination of the best elements from both my previous projects. It has a province-wide scope, but each chapter focuses on a specific activity or event. Alison and I put our heads together to come up with a list of things that we love most about Nova Scotia. This is not a "best of" list — although everything in this book is worthy of that moniker — and some people will be surprised that there is no chapter on driving the Cabot Trail or visiting the Halifax Citadel or the Town of Lunenburg, for example. Our thinking was that these destinations are so well known that they do not need any further publicity. Instead we chose places and adventures that have left a lasting impression on us and that are perhaps not so well publicized. We wanted to make sure there were chapters that represent things to do in every season, in every region and for every age and ability. We were conscious that some of the experiences in the book, such as visiting Sable Island, are prohibitively expensive for many, so we balanced that with lots of adventures that are either free or low cost.

The good news is there are myriad great things we couldn't include in this book and, if there is enough interest, we'll follow up with some of those. We welcome your suggestions.

Dale Dunlop,
Head of St. Margaret's Bay

MAP OF LOCATIONS

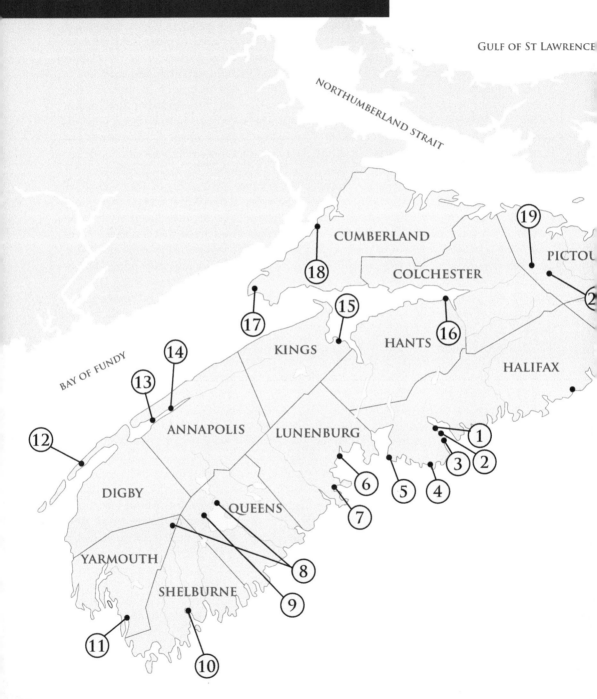

GULF OF ST LAWRENCE

NORTHUMBERLAND STRAIT

CUMBERLAND

COLCHESTER

PICTOU

(19)

(18)

(17)

(15)

(16)

KINGS

HANTS

HALIFAX

BAY OF FUNDY

(14)

(13)

ANNAPOLIS

LUNENBURG

(1)

(12)

(3)

(2)

DIGBY

(6)

(5)

(4)

QUEENS

(7)

(8)

(9)

YARMOUTH

SHELBURNE

(11)

(10)

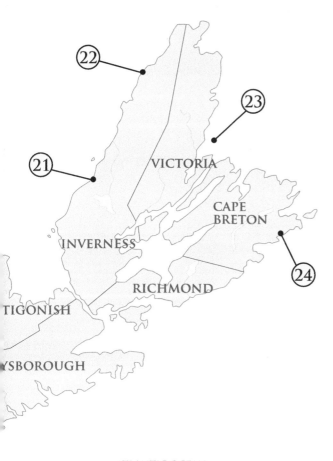

VICTORIA

CAPE
BRETON

INVERNESS

RICHMOND

TIGONISH

YSBOROUGH

ATLANTIC OCEAN

SABLE
ISLAND

BUCKET LIST LOCATIONS

1. Canadian Museum of Immigration
2. Halifax Waterfront
3. International Tattoo
4. Pennant Point
5. Peggy's Cove
6. Oak Island
7. *Bluenose II*
8. Dark Sky Preserve
9. Tobeatic Wilderness Area
10. Shelburne
11. Acadian Day
12. Digby Neck
13. Port-Royal
14. Fort Anne
15. Grand Pré
16. World's Highest Tides
17. Three Sisters
18. Glooscap Trail
19. Sugar Moon Farm
20. Gully Lake
21. Cape Breton Golf Courses
22. Skyline Trail
23. Bird Islands
24. Fortress of Louisbourg
25. Sable Island

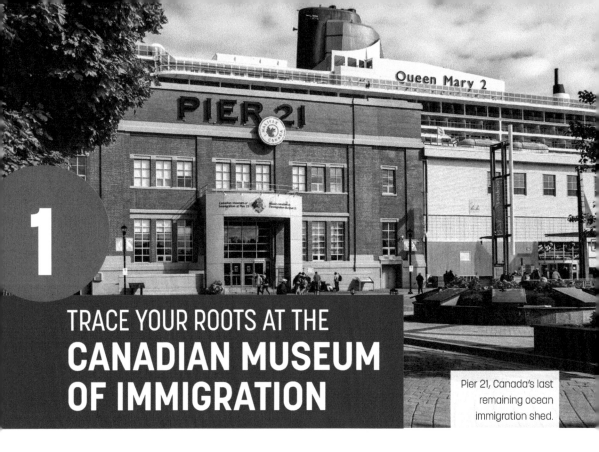

1

TRACE YOUR ROOTS AT THE
CANADIAN MUSEUM OF IMMIGRATION

Pier 21, Canada's last remaining ocean immigration shed.

Of Canada's six national museums, only two are located outside the National Capital Region: the Canadian Museum for Human Rights in Winnipeg, Manitoba, and the Canadian Museum of Immigration in Halifax. Usually referred to as Pier 21, because it is located in a portion of what once was a complex of two immense brick buildings identified by that name, it is a must-visit for all Nova Scotians and visitors alike. Between 1928 and 1971, almost one million immigrants to Canada landed by ship on the harbour side of Pier 21 and emerged through the doors as prospective Canadian citizens as they made their way by train to all parts of the country to start a new life. There were larger immigration centres, such as Quebec City where over seven million immigrants landed, but by the time anyone realized that preserving a record of how the majority of Canadians' forebears came to be here was important to our history, only Pier 21 was left standing.

It was not the Canadian government that recognized the need for an immigration museum. It was through the efforts of a few visionaries, such as Dr. Ruth Goldbloom, that Pier 21 did not suffer the same fate as all of Canada's other immigration sheds. It was designated as a national historic site in 1997 and opened as a not-for-profit museum in 1999. In 2011 the federal government stepped in and designated it as a national museum, thus ensuring its status as one of the most important places in the country.

Pier 21 is just past the southern end of the Halifax Harbourwalk, which is featured in Chapter 2, but we think it deserves its own recognition as one of Nova Scotia's must-do experiences. Firstly, the museum is Canada's version of Ellis Island and bears a striking resemblance in both design and function to that famous American melting pot. Secondly, because Canada is a nation of immigrants, almost all arriving here because they were looking for a better life, it is important to understand the commonality of our ancestors' experience. Finally, Pier 21 functions as Canada's greatest genealogy resource for persons who wish to learn more about their predecessors and how they got here. In these days of exploding interest in sites such as Ancestry.com, there are experts at Pier 21 who can help you find more information about your past in minutes than you can find in days of searching the internet (although they do use Ancestry.com as one of their tools).

The museum is open year-round with varying hours depending on the season. In summer it opens at 9:30 a.m. and closes at 5:30 p.m. In winter it opens at 10:00 a.m. and closes at 5:00 p.m. Adult admission is $14.50, with lower rates for seniors, children and students. For those arriving by motor vehicle there is a parking lot just across the street that is free on weekends and holidays. We highly recommend taking one of the guided tours that start regularly and are offered in English and French. Expect to spend about two hours touring the museum and much more if you decide to trace your roots in the genealogy section. Check out the museum's website at Pier21.ca for the most up-to-date information.

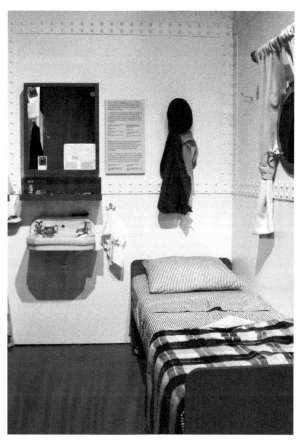

A replica cabin from a typical ocean liner carrying immigrants to Canada.

The museum is divided into three distinct permanent exhibit areas, starting with the Pier 21 Story exhibit. Here you will find a model of what Pier 21 looked like when it was fully operational and realize that the museum occupies a fraction of the space that was once required to process the million-plus immigrants who landed here. Today a number of businesses, such as Garrison Brewery, and institutions, such as the Nova Scotia College of Art and Design,

Trunks and suitcases used by immigrants to Canada.

occupy space that was once part of the Pier 21 complex.

The Pier 21 Story exhibit recreates the journey of immigrants from the time they left their home country until they were cleared to leave Pier 21 and board a train to their final destination. Most of the people who first landed at Pier 21 came by way of large passenger ships that were built for the specific purpose of ferrying people across the Atlantic or Pacific. Conditions were quite acceptable on board compared to the squalor and disease that made the trans-Atlantic crossing so deadly in the eighteenth and nineteenth centuries. Some of the most famous liners of the day, such as the *Aquitania*, brought passengers to Pier 21.

The prospective immigrants to Canada needed to have valid passports from their country of departure, pre-arranged Canadian visas and either a Canadian sponsor or a job offer awaiting them. After disembarking, the passengers would make

Visitor responses to a display asking: "What would you pack in your suitcase?"

their way to a large room where their papers would be checked and, if all was in order, they would be provided with immigration tags. The entire process usually took no longer than fifteen minutes once you got to the front of the line, which could take a couple of hours, depending upon how many people were waiting to be processed.

Many of the visitors today are descendants of parents and grandparents who first arrived in Canada at Pier 21, and they are invited to write their stories on tags similar to those that would have been issued to their relatives.

Next the immigrants would collect their luggage, which in some cases included huge wooden trunks crammed with all their worldly possessions.

Finally, the immigrants would come to a small general store where they could buy food and other supplies they would need for their onward journey. The exhibit ends with a replica 'colonist' car, similar to thousands that took the vast majority of people who landed in Halifax to other parts of the country, where they established themselves in this new land of opportunity.

On the opposite side of the museum is the Canadian Immigration Story exhibit, which paints the much larger picture of immigration to Canada. This includes some of the darker moments of our history, such as the Chinese head tax and the exclusion of certain groups as 'undesirables.'

The exhibit ends on a positive note with the Suitcase Project, where people can write down what they absolutely would have to take with them if they were to leave for another country. The notes are placed in

Visitors can write their own stories on tags similar to those that were issued to immigrants arriving at Pier 21.

tiny cardboard suitcases and pinned to the wall where later visitors can open them and read their contents. The ones from young children are fascinating.

Immigration tags.

While the first part of Pier 21 focuses on the experiences of those who came to Canada through this immigration shed and the second on immigration as a whole, the third is entirely personal. The Scotiabank Family History Centre has access to all public immigration records in North America as well as census and other vital genealogical data from around the world. Don't make the mistake of thinking that only records of those who entered Canada through Pier 21 are kept here. In fact, they have records from all North American ports of entry.

You can engage the services of an expert researcher to help you trace where, when and how your ancestors came to North America, and it's all free, although there is a charge for reproduction of records. The

Pier 21 offers interactive displays for kids.

person assisting Dale was able to identify the ship upon which his paternal grandfather arrived in the late 1800s. There is a strange feeling that comes over you when you look at a written record with the names of your forebears written on a ship's manifest or in an early British census.

Most of the recommended activities in this book are best undertaken in the summer or fall and are weather dependent, but visiting the Scotiabank Family History Centre is a great way to spend a few hours on a cold winter's day. Chances are that you will have the place to yourself, and there is no charge for visiting the genealogical portion of Pier 21.

WHAT YOU NEED TO KNOW:

Name: Canadian Museum of Immigration at Pier 21
Address: 1055 Marginal Rd, Halifax, NS B3H 4P7
Websites: pier21.ca
pier21.ca/scotiabank-family-history-centre
Season: Year-round
Opening times: Most days 10-3 p.m.
Price: <$15
Other note: Every visitor who enters is greeted by an experienced staff member ready to help you research
Classic photo op (Instagram worthy!): Discovering details from your family's past

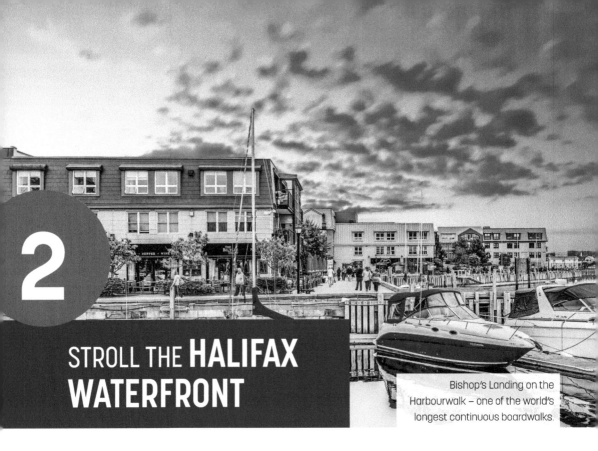

2

STROLL THE **HALIFAX WATERFRONT**

Bishop's Landing on the Harbourwalk – one of the world's longest continuous boardwalks.

Halifax was founded in 1749 by the British as a counterweight to the great French fortress at Louisbourg in Cape Breton. Its location was selected because of its large natural harbour with a massive glacial drumlin looming over it, which was eventually transformed into the Halifax Citadel. Having one of the largest ice-free harbours in the world, Halifax became the staging ground for convoys in both the First World War and the Second World War, as well as the headquarters of the Allies fighting the Battle of the Atlantic. It was the first place survivors and most of the recovered dead from the *Titanic* were landed and, in many cases, buried. In 1917 it suffered the largest non-nuclear explosion in history when a munitions ship was struck by a Norwegian relief vessel. Almost 2,000 people were killed, and the north end of the city was almost completely destroyed. For more than a million immigrants, Halifax was their first port of call on their journey to become the newest Canadians. For over 60,000 Canadians it was their last step on Canadian soil as they departed for the killing fields of the First World War and never returned. Halifax Harbour has more than its share of history, and today is the most visited tourist attraction in Nova Scotia.

However, it was not always that way. Up until fairly recently much of the harbourfront was inaccessible to the public, with a collection of decaying wharves, old warehouses, a power station and a few

The Emigrant – one of many pieces of public art along the waterfront.

government buildings fronting on what was a dirty, oily waterfront. Raw sewage was dumped into the harbour at several locations and in places the water literally stank. A group of historic buildings, dating back to the late 1700s, were designated as a national historic site in 1963. In the late 1960s and early 1970s, when city planners proposed demolishing them to make way for a new highway, Halifax citizens successfully rallied against the project. The buildings, collectively known as Historic Properties, became Canada's first major waterfront restoration project. Since then, the harbourfront has undergone a transformation to make it one of the world's best waterfront walks, with dozens of attractions for people of all ages. Always a work in progress, the Halifax Harbourwalk gets better each year as new and innovative ideas are put into action.

The waterfront stretches from the Cunard Centre in the south to Casino Nova Scotia, with four kilometres of that being waterfront boardwalk. If you are arriving by cruise ship, this will be your first taste of Halifax. While there are many interesting vendors in the cruise ship terminal, there are many more at the nearby Seaport Farmers' Market and other waterfront locations.

There are currently 60 marked attractions either on or very near the waterfront, which you will find on the many Harbourwalk maps along the route. It could easily take two days to see everything, but we prefer to come back time and again at different times of year, including winter, to get the most out of the Halifax waterfront.

We recommend starting at the south side of the walk near Pier 21 if you are arriving by motor vehicle, because it is easier to get parking here than at the other lots along the route. Also, the parking lot at Pier 21 is free on weekends and holidays, while the others are not. On days when large cruise ships are in port, the waterfront can get very crowded. Unless you are a fan of taking pictures of these ships, and many are, we recommend checking cruisehalifax.ca to see if a ship is scheduled and planning your walk on a day when you can avoid these crowds.

The Canadian Museum of Immigration at Pier 21 should be the first stop on any excursion to the waterfront. See Chapter 1 for more information about it, and check it out at Pier21.ca.

Outside the museum you will come across the first of many great pieces of public art. Stroll the waterfront to find as many of these as you can, and create a photographic record of them. This is *The Emigrant*.

The museum occupies only a small portion of the two huge brick buildings that constitute Pier 21. In the rest of the

The Halifax Seaport Farmers' Market the oldest, continuously operating farmers' market in North America.

space you will find the Nova Scotia Centre for Craft and Design, where the Mary E. Black Gallery displays the works of modern artisans working in many mediums, as well as numerous shops and restaurants. Drop in to the East Coast Lifestyle store, where the amazingly popular anchor and rope logo has made their clothing one of the hottest selling brands in Canada. Here you will also find one of Nova Scotia's first and most popular microbreweries, Garrison Brewing, where you can sample a flight of the freshest ales you'll find anywhere. If you're not a beer drinker, sample one of their Dockyard Sodas.

Next up is the Halifax Seaport Farmers' Market, which has roots going all the way back to 1750. It is now housed in a bright, airy, two-storey building that was purpose-designed to host the largest market in Nova Scotia. Here you will find a vast selection of craftspeople offering jewelry, leatherwork, woodwork, paintings, photographs and

other crafts, as well as dozens of food merchants offering both fresh fruits and vegetables, dairy products, prepared meats and fish. There is no shortage of places to try many of the cuisines that reflect Halifax's growing mix of nationalities. At last count we found over 20 places offering interesting and usually pleasantly spicy foods that at one time were unheard of in Halifax. If you have a sweet tooth, there are many types of baking and candy to be sampled. For many Haligonians, attending the Seaport Farmers' Market has become a weekly or even daily pilgrimage and is now an entrenched part of our city culture.

The Seaport Farmers' Market is not the only one in the waterfront area. On Saturdays the old and very picturesque Keith's Brewery building on Lower Water Street, just a short walk from the waterfront, hosts more than 40 vendors in a setting that purists believe better represents the spirit of a true farmers' market.

Georges Island Lighthouse. The island is the largest in Halifax Harbour.

The reality is that both markets are great for Halifax and their friendly competition is welcomed by most.

Standing between the entrance to the seaport area and the Halifax Harbourwalk, where the boardwalk begins, is a statue to one of Nova Scotia's most famous citizens, Samuel Cunard. Most people assume that he was an Englishman because the famous shipping line that bears his name is based in Great Britain. However, long before he moved to Liverpool he was running steamships out of Halifax, where he was born and raised. In 2019, to celebrate the Samuel Cunard Prize for Vision, Courage and Creativity — awarded to an individual who demonstrates the traits exemplified by Cunard during his lifetime — the *Queen Mary 2* and the *Queen Elizabeth* arrived in port on the same day. Both these trans-Atlantic ocean liners make fairly regular calls on Halifax, continuing the almost 200-year association of this celebrated ship owner with his hometown.

Next on the list of attractions is the Discovery Centre, which is one of the newest museums to open near the waterfront. It is essentially a science centre with exhibition galleries based on the ocean, flight, health and energy, all areas of research and innovation in which many world-class companies based in the metro Halifax area specialize. Children will love the Just for Kids sections, while science nerds will gravitate to the Innovation Lab. For a small extra fee, you can enter the Dome Theatre, which is a scaled down version of a planetarium using the most up-to-date technology to view the stars and planets.

After leaving the Discovery Centre you pass under the entrance to the Halifax Harbourwalk and begin a four-kilometre boardwalk — one of the longest waterfront boardwalks in the world. Nothing separates you from the glorious views of Halifax Harbour and the absolute beehive of activity taking place on both land and sea.

Tall Ships Quay during the Tall Ships Festival.

This first area of the boardwalk is called Tall Ships Quay. The name brings to mind the best time to visit the Halifax waterfront — every three to four years Halifax becomes a port of call for the Tall Ships Festival. Tall ships are remnants of the great days of sail and are among the most beautiful sights on the sea when in full sail. When they do come, there are usually at least 15 or more. Many are official training vessels for various navies around the world. Once they come in port, they are tied up along the entire boardwalk area and many, such as the United States training ship, *The Eagle*, are open for public tours. The highlight of the visit is the sail past, usually led by the iconic Nova Scotian schooner, *Bluenose II*. To see some of the largest sailing ships in the world fully decked out is something one will never forget. Keep an eye open for future dates at tallshipsnetwork.com, and make sure to mark it in the calendar.

Continuing on, you will come to the first of a number of commercial/residential complexes. Bishop's Landing has some great restaurants, interesting one-of-a-kind shops and a kids' splash pad, where 24 waterspouts offer great fun and a chance to cool off on the increasingly hot days of mid-summer.

Don't be alarmed by what appear to be a series of street lamps that have somehow become twisted into weird shapes on nearby South Battery Pier. It's a piece of whimsical art called *Got Drunk, Fell Down*.

This is one of several areas where you can purchase tickets for an excursion out onto the harbour. The Harbour Hopper, which is a huge amphibious vehicle, takes a ride through downtown and uptown Halifax and then a short cruise up and down the waterfront. It is a strange feeling to be sitting on dry

Just offshore is Georges Island, with its honeycomb of fortifications and one of the many lighthouses that help mariners safely make their way into or out of port.

Aside from fishing boats, you might see some of the largest ships in the world making their way to one of the two container piers, naval vessels, sometimes including submarines and aircraft carriers, cruise ships of all sizes and of course, lots of pleasure craft, from sea kayaks to gigantic ocean-going yachts.

Theodore Tugboat and HMCS *Sackville* – Canada's oldest warship.

land one minute and then plunging down a ramp into the ocean. This is one of Halifax's most popular marine excursions. (For tour times and tickets, visit: Ambassatours.com/family-fun-adventure.)

For a more sedate experience, you can board an old-fashioned paddle wheeler and enjoy an extended trip on the harbour, or you can board the *Silva* and experience sailing on a tall ship. Other tours take people out to the mouth of the harbour, past three lighthouses, looking for whales, dolphins, sunfish and other marine life. A smaller boat takes groups out to sea, where you can fish for cod, mackerel, pollock and other species that frequent the outer harbour. For children, the must-do harbour trip is on *Theodore Tugboat* as he tours the sites of Big Harbour and brings the TV series that has been viewed in over 80 countries to life.

Most of the boat tours last anywhere from 30 minutes (*Theodore Tugboat*) to three hours (deep-sea fishing). If you are interested in being on the water at sunset, there are dinner cruises and dedicated party boats to accommodate all levels of revelry. You can also take a water taxi to McNabs Island, which at the beginning of the 20th century was a top destination for weekend excursions. Today it is a quiet place to explore a number of abandoned forts or walk the beach where British navy deserters were once hung in gibbets. Lastly, if you want to do it yourself, you can rent a sea kayak or even a Jet Ski to tour the harbour at your own pace. Bicycles and Segways are also available for rent on the boardwalk, although the latter requires going on a guided tour.

Just after Bishop's Landing there is a set of beach volleyball courts where, at times,

The Wave sculpture at Sackville Landing.

you might see some of the best players in North America competing. Next is Vendor's Village, featuring a couple dozen seasonal sales outlets. If you haven't been shopped out at the Seaport Farmer's Market, there is plenty to tempt one here.

Behind it is Summit Place, where in 1995 the G7 met along with Mikhail Gorbachev. One of the most beloved statues on the waterfront is at Sackville Landing, which abuts Summit Place. It is called *The Sailor Statue*, and represents the hundreds of thousands of Canadians who have served in the Canadian navy. For us, it represents the very essence of Halifax as Canada's naval city.

Sackville Landing features another great work of public art. Once controversial and now a prime meeting spot on the waterfront, *The Wave* has to be the subject of the most

disobeyed sign in Canada. Even though there is an express prohibition from climbing it, nobody pays any attention. A few years after it was erected the city gave up and surrounded it with rubber matting, but the sign is still there.

Right behind *The Wave* is the most popular playground in Halifax, with a large orange, not yellow, submarine being the main feature. The Visitor Information Centre located here is where you can get all the information you might want about other places to explore in Halifax and beyond.

Passing the Visitor Centre you will notice two older-looking ships moored at the waterfront and a number of very large anchors. This is the bailiwick of the Maritime Museum of the Atlantic, the crown jewel of the Nova Scotia museum collection. This is an absolute must-visit attraction on the

A deck chair from RMS *Titanic,* on display in the Maritime Museum of the Atlantic *Titanic* exhibit.

waterfront, and you should allot at least a couple of hours to visit it and the two ships associated with it. Inside the museum you will find permanent exhibits on the *Titanic* (including one of its famous deck chairs), the Halifax Explosion, famous Nova Scotia shipwrecks and the treasure hunters who have found them, as well as Age of Sail and Age of Steam galleries, a model of Theodore Tugboat's Big Harbour, a ship chandler's store, dozens of ship models and much more.

Outside you can go aboard the last remaining corvette from the Second World War, the HMCS *Sackville*. Corvettes were specifically built to escort convoys leaving Halifax and other ports, taking much needed war materials for Europe. All told, 123 were built and only the *Sackville* has survived.

Make sure to go aboard and get a feeling of what it was like to cross the rough North Atlantic over and over again under the relentless pursuit of German U-boats.

Visit the CSS *Acadia*, a survey vessel that has the distinction of being the only ship to serve in both world wars and to survive the Halifax Explosion — now that's a survivor! At the end of the Museum Wharf, where the *Acadia* is docked, is an interesting and moving monument to the hundreds of thousands of Canadians who departed the Halifax waterfront to serve on the Western Front in the First World War. It is a memorial arch called *The Last Steps* and is a companion to a similar arch at Passchendaele, Belgium, where 16,000 Canadians were killed or wounded. Of the

Nova Scotian Crystal, Canada's first and only hand-blown crystal factory.

Crystal being prepared at Nova Scotian Crystal.

connects the Museum Wharf with Murphy's Cable Wharf. Trust us, if the sea bridge gets hit with the wake of a passing ship it will rock like crazy and you'll get a pretty good idea of what it's like to be at sea in rough weather. By the time you get to the other side you might not have your 'sea legs' and literally stagger like a drunken sailor as you land on solid ground. This is a temporary structure put up to accommodate the large construction project at Queen's Marque, but it is so popular we expect it will become permanent.

Murphy's Cable Wharf is home to Murphy's on the Water, the largest building located on a pier along the waterfront with a very large restaurant and souvenir shop. It's also where a number of the boat cruises mentioned above depart.

Leaving the Cable Wharf you arrive at Chebucto Landing, where the clock tower is a popular meeting spot to start rambles along

more than 300,000 Canadians who departed from Halifax, over 60,000 never returned and took their last steps on Canadian soil on the Halifax waterfront.

Right beside *The Last Steps* is the Sea Bridge, a long floating wooden structure that

A Halifax Busker Festival performer.

the waterfront. Here you will find the most unique shop on the waterfront and, in fact, one that is unique in Canada. Nova Scotian Crystal was founded over two decades ago by Nova Scotians with Irish roots who imported trained glass blowers from the world famous Waterford Crystal Factory to start Canada's only true hand-blown crystal establishment. All items are made on site and you are welcome to watch the artisans at work. Their designs have been recognized throughout the world for their originality and quality. They have a legion of loyal customers, including us. When it looked like the business might fail after the 2008 recession, when luxury goods were not a priority item for many, their customers rallied and bought enough crystal to save the company. It is now thriving again. Anything from Nova Scotian Crystal makes a wonderful souvenir of your visit to the waterfront. Their wares are not cheap, but quality never is.

At Chebucto Landing you can embark on another marine adventure at a price that won't affect your wallet. For $2.50 you can board the Dartmouth Ferry, the oldest ferry service in North America and second in the world only to the famous ferry across the Mersey River in Liverpool, England. In operation since 1752, it will take you to

Historic Properties, home to ten of the oldest buildings in Halifax.

Dartmouth, which is as old as Halifax and has an interesting historical area to explore. The ferry ride provides fabulous views of the Halifax and Dartmouth waterfronts as well as Georges Island and the navy yards. Take the ferry to Alderney Landing, which has its share of good restaurants and shops, and walk the three-kilometre Dartmouth Harbourfront Trail to the Woodside Ferry Terminal, where you can return to Chebucto Landing.

Right beside the Ferry Terminal you will come across a small amphitheatre which, at the right time of year, is the most exciting place to be on the waterfront. For a week every summer it is the primary spot for viewing the many acts that constitute the Halifax Busker Festival. Buskers are street performers who entertain in exchange for voluntary donations, and they include acrobats, magicians, comedians, jugglers and musicians. The level of talent is outstanding, and over the three decades that Halifax has been hosting buskers, acts have come from all over the world to showcase their abilities. In 2019, 15 acts put on over 300 shows, so there's no excuse for not taking in at least a few. There are now a number of busker festivals throughout Canada, but Halifax was the first and has venues like the waterfront that can't be beaten. If you are planning a visit to Halifax, make sure to go online (buskers.ca) and get the dates for the next year's event.

Now you come at last to the place where it all started, Historic Properties, which first opened to the public in the 1970s. You will find ten of the oldest buildings in Halifax, of which seven are a designated national historic site. The buildings are constructed of

The Halifax Harbour ferry service.

wood and stone, with the oldest dating back to the late 1700s.

The most famous are undoubtedly those that make up Privateers' Wharf (also called Historic Properties), which was once the departure point for many of the famous privateer vessels that preyed upon American shipping during the War of 1812. Returning to Halifax laden with booty, the privateers made many Haligonian investors rich, including Enos Collins, who founded a bank with the proceeds — now called CIBC. This is also the place Stan Rogers was referring to when he wrote perhaps his most famous song, "Barrett's Privateers."

Historic Properties today is a collection of business offices, such as Parks Canada, high end clothiers, souvenir shops, a gastropub and a number of restaurants. It is a favourite spot for *al fresco* dining on the waterfront.

By now anyone who has taken in most of what there is to see and do will be exhausted and will welcome the chance to sit in one of the deck chairs that line the waterfront just after Historic Properties. This is the end point for this wonderful walk and is a great place to rest and recover your energy.

USEFUL WEBSITES:

pier21.ca
cruisehalifax.ca
halifaxfarmersmarket.com
thediscoverycentre.ca
tallshipsnetwork.com
ambassatours.com
maritimemuseum.novascotia.ca
novascotiancrystal.com
buskers.ca
historicproperties.ca

3

ATTEND THE ROYAL NOVA SCOTIA
INTERNATIONAL TATTOO

Almost every experience in this book takes place in the great outdoors, with a notable exception in our recommendation to take in the largest indoor military tattoo in the world, the Royal Nova Scotia International Tattoo. Ever since its foundation in 1976, it has been one of the most popular annual events in the province. It draws in busloads of tourists from around the world to the Scotiabank Centre during its week-long run that starts in late June and runs through Canada Day weekend. It kicks off the beginning of the summer festival season in Halifax, with outdoor band concerts and parades in addition to the indoor performances, and puts Haligonians in a great frame of mind after a long winter and spring.

So what exactly is a military tattoo? Well it's definitely not body art on a sailor's arm. The word is derived from the Dutch words *tap toe* — first used to describe a ritual at 9:30 each evening when a drummer would parade through the streets and beat a cadence that told bartenders to turn off the taps and for the soldiers drinking in their establishments to return to their barracks. Later the drum was replaced by a bugle and the word was anglicized into tattoo. It still exists as a recognized bugle call in the British and United States armed forces. Beginning in the 19th century, more elaborate musical endeavours evolved into full-blown displays that melded music with drills and other forms of military precision put on to impress

Tattoo performers, on stage.

upon the public that indeed, they were in good hands.

The other thing a tattoo is definitely not, is a celebration of war or militarism. In fact, it's the opposite, with a focus on remembrance, sacrifice and public service.

In 1976 Colonel Ian Fraser, who had great experience organizing tattoos for the Canadian military, was asked to put one on to mark the visit of the Queen Mother to Halifax during the International Gathering of the Clans. He did such a great job that it became an annual event that has evolved into a mainstay of Halifax's tourism scene and, just as importantly, an opportunity for thousands of Nova Scotians to participate as volunteers or, even better, performers. Playing a part in the tattoo has almost become a rite of passage for young dancers, gymnasts and musicians from all over the province. In 2006, on the occasion of Queen Elizabeth's 80th birthday, it received the designation 'Royal.' The 'international' in the name stems from the

fact that every year performers from all over the world take part in the show. During the 2019 tattoo, which we attended, there were performers from many Canadian provinces, the United States, Great Britain, Germany, Australia, Japan and Estonia. Up to 2,000 people perform annually at the Royal Nova Scotia International Tattoo — that's a lot of people under one roof, and boy do they put on a show.

Each show runs for two and a half hours with a 20-minute intermission. Each act usually only lasts two to three minutes so that the show moves at a very quick pace and even small children won't get bored. The show opens with a huge musical splash that features the largest choir you'll probably ever see on stage at once (or, more accurately, arced above the entrance to the floor of the arena) while one band after another, all decked out in colourful and contrasting uniforms, marches out into view until the entire floor is one giant musical collage. It's a sight you'll never forget.

Pipe, drum, band, dance, acrobatic and drill performances are annual Tattoo features.

Every year the tattoo features a different theme. In 2019 the theme was the Power of Peace, and it commemorated the 75th anniversary of D-Day and the 30th anniversary of the fall of the Berlin Wall, events leading to the end of a hot war and a cold one and ushering in an era of peace.

What types of acts might you expect to see at the tattoo? We've often heard the analogy of the tattoo being part Cirque du Soleil, part ceilidh and part marching band, which is a little too simplistic. There will certainly be some amazing gymnastic acts of the type made famous by Quebec's Cirque du Soleil, and there will be Highland dancers and fiddlers and some great marching bands. However, there will also be massed pipes and drums on a scale seen nowhere else under one roof. The sound of over 100 kilted bagpipers followed by massive bass drums is something no one will ever forget. You can feel it in your bones, and the music

creates an emotional intensity in the arena that must be experienced in person to be understood.

On the military side, there will always be a competition between two or more of the armed forces bases in Atlantic Canada. It may be a gun run, in which naval squadrons compete to dismantle and transport a field gun over an obstacle course in the shortest period of time. Or it could be a Jiffy Jeep competition between army units to dismantle and reassemble an actual working jeep. These competitions might not sound overly exciting, but to the spectators these are among the highlights of the tattoo and the rivalry between the army and navy units is very apparent. Keeping with the military theme, precision drill units put on a show that must take years of practice to master. In 2019 the United States Air Force Drill Team used rifles with razor sharp bayonets to create a whirling gauntlet through which

The RCMP National Ceremonial Troop, often featured at the Tattoo.

the drill sergeant walked without blinking or wavering as the audience cringed in disbelief.

Every tattoo is different and over the years has featured the famed United States Marine Band, the Flying Grandpas, the Japanese Maritime Self-Defence Force Band and many other unique acts.

The presence of close to 2,000 tattoo performers in Halifax for a week transforms the city. Brass bands, pipe and drum bands and drill units march in the Canada Day parade and put on concerts at various venues around the city, including the Public Gardens, Victoria Park and the waterfront. With all the people dressed in the uniforms of many different nations, the city streets take on a look that harkens back to the days when Halifax was truly the Warden of the North, garrisoned by troops from all over the British Empire.

Attending the Royal Nova Scotia International Tattoo is a must if you are to claim to have seen the best the province has to offer.

WHAT YOU NEED TO KNOW:
Name: Royal Nova Scotia International Tattoo
Address: Scotiabank Centre, 1800 Argyle St, Halifax, NS B3J 2V9
Website: nstattoo.ca
Season: Summer
Opening times: 8 days at the end of June/early July
Price: Tickets cost between $32 and $75 for adults
Other note: Kids are free
Classic photo op (Instagram worthy!): The spectacle of an arena full of performers

4

HIKE TO
PENNANT POINT

Circular Cove on the
Pennant Point Trail.

We have used many modes of active transportation over the years to explore Nova Scotia, including cycling, kayaking, canoeing, cross-country skiing, snowshoeing and just plain walking. However, if we had to choose one method, it would almost certainly be hiking — and by that we mean getting out on a defined trail that has plenty of elevation change and enough distance to present a challenge that will get the heart racing and give the legs a good workout. There are many trails across this province that provide a range in levels of difficulty and reward that challenge with incredible views. For this book, we selected two trails that anyone with a reasonable level of fitness should be able to complete: the Skyline Trail and Pennant

Point. Read Chapter 22 for more about why we chose the Skyline Trail.

Why Pennant Point? There are multiple reasons we think this is the ideal hike, starting with the fact it is accessible to a large segment of the population. It also has amazing scenery that includes classic Atlantic coast granite rocks meeting the sea. In certain conditions this can lead to spectacular surf and crashing waves. If you want to get the perfect photo of sea spraying high into the air, this is the trail to do it on. There are great views of Sambro Island, with its famous lighthouse whose foundations were laid in 1759 and from where Joshua Slocum set sail in the tiny sloop *Spray* to become the first man to solo navigate the globe in 1895.

A peregrine falcon spotted on the trail.

Bog cranberries, ripe for picking.

The Pennant Point hike passes through various ecosystems, which contain a great variety of flora and fauna. Depending on the time of year, you may see a carpet of blue flag iris or hundreds of carnivorous pitcher plants mixed in with bog cranberries and blueberries for the picking.

Careful observers can spot up to a dozen species of orchid, including some that are quite rare. Looking up, especially in the spring and early fall, you will see a great variety of birds migrating north or south. On our most recent hike, we came across a flock of whimbrels and a peregrine falcon that posed on a nearby rock.

On the seaward side, expect to see eiders, scoters, cormorants and occasionally gannets, along with various species of gulls and terns. Out to sea, it's quite common to see container ships, ocean liners and other large vessels making their way in and out of Halifax Harbour, along with smaller pleasure craft beating their way into the wind at a

Alison sporting her hiking poles, useful for the rockier sections.

Blue flag iris along the trail in early summer..

experienced and novice hikers alike. Firstly, the trail is quite well marked. Although in places it goes for a considerable distance over bare rock, and it might not be obvious where the trail recommences once the end of the rocks is reached, someone has been kind enough to spray paint blue markings on the rocks to indicate the proper path. There's little risk of getting lost. Secondly, you don't have to go all the way to Pennant Point to enjoy this hike; in fact, most people don't make it to the end. For families with small children or those who might not be in the most fit condition, you can decide where to turn around and head back. We've seen many groups over the years that like to pick out a nice location on the rocks and have a picnic by the sea or do some beachcombing in one of the small coves that dot this part of the coast. Although there are parts of the trail that go through the forest, especially at the

precariously slow rate. This coast has seen more than its share of shipwrecks. Lastly, if you are lucky you might see any one of a number of species of whales that regularly migrate along the Atlantic coast of Nova Scotia. You definitely don't want to leave your binoculars behind on this hike.

In addition to what there is to see on a hike to Pennant Point, there are a number of other factors that make this a great choice for

Classic scenery along the trail where Atlantic coast granite rocks meets the sea.

beginning, most of the walking is near the ocean, and that means a constant breeze that keeps biting insects at bay — a real bonus, particularly in blackfly season.

Because this is a real hike and not a stroll in the park, you need to be prepared. We recommend that each hiker take a day pack with plenty of water, sunscreen, a hat that covers the ears, a walking stick (there are a few places where these are invaluable as a brace, especially going downhill or over boulders), a cell phone (coverage is pretty good and you have access to the GPS function with Google Maps) and something to snack on. Proper footwear is also a necessity, as there are many places where it would be easy to turn an ankle or worse. Waterproof hiking boots are best, although when it's quite dry you might get by with sneakers. Definitely do not wear

sandals or flip flops. Obviously, cameras and binoculars are not necessary, but will greatly enhance the experience, although these days most people use phones to take pictures.

One of the strangest things about the Pennant Point Trail is that nobody seems to agree on how long it is. The Nova Scotia Parks website puts it at 10 kilometres, or roughly 6 miles each way. That is repeated on the Nova Scotia Hiking website. However, on a site that uses Google Maps it comes in at just 4.5 kilometres each way, which we believe is much more accurate. On our most recent hike we used an app that measured our total steps from the parking lot to Pennant Point and back and it came to just under 12.5 kilometres or 7.75 miles. Considering that this included some short side trips to lookoff points, coves etc., we believe the Pennant Point Trail is a lot shorter than the 'official'

33

Thistles with Fritillary butterflies.

You get to Sambro from Halifax on Highway 306 and turn left where it ends at Highway 349, which will take about 30 minutes in typical traffic. From here follow the signs to Crystal Crescent, turning left onto Sambro Creek Road, which is a dirt road, and then right onto Crystal Crescent Road. For some reason this last turn is not signed, and the road to the beach has been infamously rough for the last 30 years. Despite the popularity of Crystal Crescent, the province has never paved the last mile or two, so prepare to be bounced around before reaching the parking lot. Here you will find the only toilets in the area, and they are pretty gross.

The parking lot is just behind the first of three beaches that collectively make up the provincial park. A boardwalk on the right side of the beach marks the beginning of the trail. The boardwalk continues past the second beach and ends after 1.3 kilometres at Mackerel Cove, which is also known as Crystal Crescent Naturist Beach. Yes, this

website would have the public believe. That's unfortunate because it no doubt deters many people from even attempting it.

The trail is accessed from Crystal Crescent Beach Provincial Park, which is not far from the fishing village of Sambro.

A wooded trail section. Most of the trail is open to the elements.

is Halifax's famous nude beach and it's not unusual to see naturists in all their glory on this section of the trail. The end of the boardwalk marks the true beginning of the Pennant Point Trail. It starts out with a fairly rough section through the woods, but once you complete this section, which is less than a kilometre, almost all the rest of the walking is in wide open spaces.

This is where you will start to see the collision between land and sea that creates one of the most iconic vistas in Nova Scotia. Also, one of the most dangerous. By all means enjoy the scene, but please do it from a safe distance, as the sea may look calm, but you never know when a rogue wave might hit, and you would not be the first one not to return from this hike.

There is something exhilarating about breathing the salt air, listening to the cries of the seabirds amidst the crash of the waves and, on a sunny day, being dazzled by the brilliant whiteness of the granite and the blues and greens of the ocean. You feel an almost hyper-sense of being alive and happy to witness this meeting of land and sea. Every Nova Scotian should stand in a spot like this on a beautiful summer or autumn day and think of the first line from our provincial song, "Farewell to Nova Scotia, the sea bound coast," and you will understand why there is such a bond between us and the sea.

Land and sea on the Pennant Point trail.

There are a number of small coves on the way to Pennant Point that are often crammed with driftwood and other detritus of the sea. You might get lucky and find one of those colourful wooden buoys used to mark lobster traps or maybe some nicely polished beach glass.

As you near Pennant Point you will see the remnants of an ancient wharf that has somehow been carried hundreds of feet inland by what must have been one very powerful storm, perhaps not unlike Hurricane Dorian that struck in 2019. What is doubly amazing about this piece of wreckage is the massive size of the wooden timbers, which clearly came from old-growth trees, the likes of which we don't see any more except in a few too rare places. Looking at it makes one think about what "the forest primeval" must have looked like when the first Europeans arrived and transformed the landscape completely. Also, in this area near the end of the trail, you come upon the opposite of the old growth trees that were used to make that wharf. The living trees in this area are stunted and the branches bearing fir all face inland in what is referred to as a krummholz forest. Newfoundlanders call it tuckamore. The trees are so gnarled that it gives the forest an aura of evil enchantment right out of a Grimms' fairy tale.

At last Pennant Point comes into view, with the krummholz forest on its edge.

To get there you have two choices — follow the trail in a large arc to avoid the huge boulder–strewn beach that separates the point from the rest of the coastline or say 'To heck with it' and pick your way through the boulders as we did on our last visit.

Once you get to the tip of Pennant Point

Boulders at Pennant Point.

you can see the villages of East and West Pennant in the distance. It is possible to follow the coastline here almost as far as East Pennant, but the trail is nowhere near as well marked and you will have to cut across the peninsula at some point through the forest. We do not recommend doing this. Nor do we recommend trying to find the old road that used to run down the spine of the peninsula. This is a very wet and frankly boring way to go back. By retracing your steps the way you came, you get a completely different perspective on the way back that almost makes it seem like you are on a different trail. Another alternative we have done is to take two cars and leave one at East Pennant and one at Crystal Crescent. This sounds like a good idea, but actually the scenery on the inward side of Pennant Point is not as interesting as that on the open Atlantic side.

We think this trail should be on every Nova Scotian's bucket list and every visitor to our province should make some time to experience this landscape at least once — just remember not to stare at the naturists.

WHAT YOU NEED TO KNOW:

Name: Pennant Point Hike
Address: Crystal Crescent Beach Provincial Park, 220 Sambro Creek Rd, Sambro Creek, NS B3V 1L8
Website: bit.ly/3cgBVyl halifaxtrails.ca/crystal-crescent
Season: Year-round
Opening times: Every day; 8 a.m.–11 p.m.
Price: Free
Other note: Wear appropriate footwear for a hike
Classic photo op (Instagram worthy!): Sea spraying high into the air

5

AVOID THE CROWDS AT
PEGGY'S COVE

Peggy's Cove Lighthouse,
in December.

Without doubt, Peggy's Cove or more particularly the Peggy's Cove Lighthouse is the
most iconic symbol of Nova Scotia in the
minds of Nova Scotians, visitors to this province and even people who have never come
within 1,000 kilometres of our coastline.
It easily rivals Lake Louise, the CN Tower
and Niagara Falls as the most photographed
place in Canada and appears on countless
calendars, postcards, jigsaw puzzles and
other tourist memorabilia sold throughout
Atlantic Canada and beyond. And there's
a good reason for this — there is nothing
else like the Peggy's Cove Lighthouse (also
called Peggy's Point Lighthouse). Sitting on
what appears from afar to be a lonely patch
of barren granite that dips into the sea at the
right angle to create the perfect sea spray, and
acting as a beacon for unwary sailors, it epito-
mizes the spirit of Nova Scotia, where land
and sea come together in perfect union, if
not always harmony. Add to that the impossibly narrow opening that leads into Peggy's
Cove, with the fishing shacks on stilts, the
paraphernalia of the lobster fishers strewn
about upon the rickety wharves and the
colourful dories and buoys and you've got an
irresistible tourist magnet. What also can't be
overlooked is the fact that Peggy's Cove is
not some remote place that takes a full day's
drive to get there but is readily accessible
from downtown Halifax on a pretty decent,
if winding, road. There's the rub. It's too easy
to get to.

According to Tourism Nova Scotia, over 2.4 million non-resident visitors came to the province in 2017 and again in 2018. These were record numbers, largely driven by the dramatic increase in cruise ship traffic the province has experienced in the last decade. Every one of these cruise ships docks in Halifax and guess where many if not most of them want to go on a day trip? Driving in to Halifax from our home in St. Margaret's Bay, we would pass sometimes as many as 30 tour buses, all filled to capacity, heading to Peggy's Cove. Add to that the many tourists who arrive in their own cars, plus the locals who, despite the hordes, still venture to see the lighthouse at least once a year, and you've got a recipe for congestion. Peggy's Cove has become our version of Venice and Dubrovnik — all iconic locations that are being loved to death. Considering that Peggy's Cove has only 30 permanent residents, the ratio of tourists to residents is actually far higher there than in either of those two beleaguered European cities.

Now we are not suggesting that anyone forego a visit to Peggy's Cove. There are a number of strategies for getting the most out of a visit, even at the busiest times of the year. But most Nova Scotians live within two hours of Peggy's Cove and can avoid the tourist crowds by visiting out of season.

As counterintuitive as it sounds, the best time of year to visit Peggy's Cove is in winter. Not just any winter day, but one where the sun is shining, the sky is bright and the wind is not howling. There are more of these days than one might think. The winter air has a clarity to it that is not present at any other time and the islands of St. Margaret's Bay and the Aspotogan Peninsula directly across from Peggy's Cove appear to be much closer

St. John's Anglican Church, Peggy's Cove, built in 1893.

than they are. They are the closest things to a mirage that we have seen in Nova Scotia and lend a magical aura to the entire area. The most likely reason is that cold air cannot hold as much moisture as warm air so in winter the sky appears a deeper blue than in summer. The fact that there are not a lot of idling tourist buses doesn't hurt either.

Contrast this scene to what you might expect to see during peak season, when parking at any one of the lots at Peggy's Cove can be next to impossible to find. We have seen vehicles parked alongside Highway 333 up to a kilometre away from the entrance road. Having the place almost to yourself creates an entirely different Peggy's Cove experience. Yes, the tourist shops will be closed, but the Sou'Wester Restaurant stays open year-round so you can drop in and warm up if you find it gets too cold.

The 200-year-old Peggy's Cove fishing village.

Visiting in winter also allows for the chance to see lobster fishers in action, as the season on the South Shore runs throughout the winter months. There are traps set just offshore and, although they are checked more frequently at the beginning and end of the season, if it is a nice day chances are good that you will see one of the classic Cape

Lobster season runs from the end of November to May 31 in this part of Nova Scotia.

Islander boats from the rocks at Peggy's Cove. What could be more Nova Scotian than that?

Once you are finished taking pictures of the lighthouse it's time to move on and explore the village with its red and white church, and the tiny cove where the wharves will be deserted, and you can get more great photos of lobster traps and buoys.

The other possibility for avoiding the crowds is to stay in one of the few little B&Bs right in the village and be there when pretty well everyone else has left, but these book up fast. Our preference in summer or fall is to stay at nearby Oceanstone Seaside Resort (oceanstoneresort.com), from where you can easily get to Peggy's Cove for sunrise or sundown. Their restaurant, Rhubarb (rhubarbrestaurant.ca), is, in our opinion, the best on the entire Peggy's Cove loop. While a bit out of the way to go from Halifax, it's great fun once a year to book one of the resort's cottages to retire to after a great meal there.

The Peggy's Cove Preservation Area barrens.

Another way to enjoy the Peggy's Cove region is to head out on your own on one of the many trails that crisscross the Peggy's Cove Preservation Area, which begins just past the hamlet of West Dover and extends beyond the Swissair Monument near the Whale's Back rock formation. Even without the lighthouse and village this is a unique landscape noted for its many glacial erratics, cranberry bogs and wonderful wildflowers. We often get in the car and head to a section of the Preservation Area we have never explored before and strike out with no destination in mind. One of the more interesting trails starts behind the West Dover ballfield and heads inland. Other trails head down to the shoreline, where you'll find brightly coloured rockweed and offshore erratics.

Finally, don't be afraid to turn off onto one of the many side roads that lead off from Highway 333 and see where they take you. Paddy's Head Lighthouse, for example, is not that far from Peggy's Cove.

The bottom line is that Peggy's Cove is beautiful at any time of year and it is possible to enjoy it without hundreds of other people trying to do the same thing at the same time. Whether you live in Nova Scotia or are visiting for a short time, with some creative thinking and the tips we've shared above, you should be able to enjoy this iconic location in relative peace.

WHAT YOU NEED TO KNOW:

Name: Peggy's Cove
Address: Peggy's Point Lighthouse, 185 Peggy's Point Road, Peggys Cove, NS
Websites: peggys-cove.com oceanstoneresort.com rhubarbrestaurant.ca
Season: Year-round
Opening times: Every day
Price: Free
Other note: Stay off the black rocks!
Classic photo op (Instagram worthy!): Iconic blue-sky view of the lighthouse

6

TOUR
OAK ISLAND

An aerial view of Oak Island from the northeast.

Oak Island, the tiny chunk of land in Mahone Bay, has been the site of probably the most famous treasure hunt in the world for over 200 years. The runaway success of the History channel's *The Curse of Oak Island* has solidified Oak Island's reputation as a place of great mystery and potentially earth-shattering discoveries — at least if any of the wild theories about what is buried there turned out to be true. It is a place that every local and visitor to Nova Scotia should visit at least once, perhaps after binge watching the TV show. However, as has been the case for decades, admission to Oak Island is strictly controlled and you might have to wait a year or more to get on an organized tour. But if you do get on, there's a fair chance that

you might see an episode of the show being filmed and perhaps even meet Marty and Rick Lagina, the stars of the series, as we did on our last visit.

The facts surrounding the discovery of a potential treasure site are themselves now a matter of legend and there is no contemporary documentation available. The story goes that in 1795 three teenagers were visiting the island and found a depression in the ground under a large oak tree and observed a pulley or block and tackle hanging from a limb of the tree. They assumed it must mean that something important had been buried here and went to get shovels to dig with. Why anyone would leave behind such obvious signs of a burial remains an

The production crew filming *The Curse of Oak Island.*

enigma. The bottom line is that neither the initial treasure seekers nor scores of others have found anything of real value on Oak Island in the 219 years that the hunt has been on. What they have found has become one of the world's greatest mysteries — a series of engineered shafts that go down to depths still unknown, false beaches and incredibly complex drainage systems that long ago dispelled any suggestion that this was simply buried treasure. Somebody with amazing resources and engineering skills must have spent months at least on the island building this system to protect or hide something, but what?

There are more theories on what may be hidden on Oak Island than on who wrote Shakespeare's plays and, in fact, Shakespeare's plays is one of the theories. Others involve any number of countries hiding something they thought could be lost to other countries if not secreted, such as the treasure of the Knights Templar and, our personal favourite, the Holy Grail. Since the area was settled not long after Halifax was founded in 1749, it seems to be common sense that it must have occurred before then, as such an undertaking could not have gone unnoticed once settlers and fishermen started to frequent the area.

George Burden and Dale with the cast of *The Curse of Oak Island.*

Getting onto Oak Island is technically easy — it is connected to the mainland by a small causeway at the end of a short paved road that branches off Highway 3 in the community of Western Shore south of Chester. However, for the past 30 or 40 years the treasure-mad owners of the island have kept public access to a minimum. There have been years where no one was allowed on

A cannon, salvaged from a Sable Island shipwreck, at the entrance to the causeway.

except the treasure seekers. It was during one of these periods in the 1970s that Dale's desire to visit Oak Island was partially satisfied when he sneaked onto the island and made a clandestine visit. At that time there were no permanent residents and the workers returned to the mainland after their shifts. He remembers the feeling of trepidation he had as he slinked across the causeway in a stooped-over scurry. He remembers more the feeling of crushing disappointment on arriving at what he thought was the Money Pit. Stupidly expecting to see the giant oak tree with a shaft underneath it, he saw instead an industrial mess of broken and rusted machinery amid a huge excavation, partially filled with water. There was nothing

romantic whatsoever about what had taken place here — it was a mess. He returned to the mainland disillusioned, but that didn't stop him from reading every new book about Oak Island that came out or following the sporadic reports of new finds on the island.

Since 1967 the late Dan Blankenship and David Tobias owned most of the island under the corporate name Triton Alliance. About 20 years ago the then-quarrelsome owners decided to sell it, and offered it to the province for about $15 million. Surprisingly, despite it being a popular (and largely inaccessible) tourist destination, the province declined the offer. In 2006, Tobias sold his interest to Michigan brothers Rick and Marty Lagina, and they and the

The replica of the Direction Stone, reportedly found buried deep in the money pit.

Blankenship interests now operate as Oak Island Tours Inc.

They have done three good things. First, they have brought a new supply of money, ideas and enthusiasm to the project and serious efforts to get to the bottom of the mystery are once again underway. Second, in collaboration with the Friends of Oak Island they have reopened the island to the public on a limited basis, with guided tours offered for a very reasonable fee every second weekend or so. Third, the Lagina brothers have made themselves into reality TV stars with *The Curse of Oak Island* on the History channel. The first season's episodes launched in January 2014 and were such a success that it went on through multiple seasons. This has led to a greater interest and desire to visit Oak Island across North America, which is a great thing for Nova Scotia tourism. It also means there are far more people wanting to visit than the tours, which take up to 50 people, can accommodate. Thus, do not expect to sign up for the next tour. You might have to wait over a year to get a successful online booking, which you can do via Eventbrite (or follow the Friends of Oak Island Society on Facebook: Facebook.com/friendsofoakisland).

Fortunately, we had the opportunity to avoid the wait and were part of a private tour, but the tour we were given was exactly the same as that offered to the public.

What brought us to Oak Island was an invitation from our friend Dr. George Burden to join a tour put on especially for

Smith's Cove, on the south side of Oak Island, looking out across Mahone Bay.

the Freemasons. Despite the fact that Dale's grandfather, father and one son are/were Masons, he never joined, although he has always been fascinated by Masonic symbolism and the powerful role that the Masons have played in US politics. However, George is a Freemason and was given permission to invite us. The Masons have always had a keen affinity for all things related to Oak Island as it apparently abounds with Masonic symbols. They also have a relationship with the fabled Knights Templar, who became one of the wealthiest Christian organizations at

the time of the Crusades, but eventually fell afoul of the king of France and the leaders were executed and much wealth confiscated by the greedy King Philip IV. However, almost from the time of dissolution in 1312 there were rumours of vast hidden stores of Templar treasure somewhere. Today there is a specific branch of Freemasonry that is called the Knights Templar and open only to Christians, as opposed to other branches that require only a belief in a supreme being.

The connection to Oak Island and the Knights Templar comes through the

somewhat murky and controversial Sir Henry Sinclair, who, while definitely a real person, has had Paul Bunyanesque exploits attributed to him. There are many things that connect Sinclair very tenuously to Oak Island, namely the belief by some that he ventured to North America, and in particular Nova Scotia, over 100 years before Columbus. We have written about this in *Exploring Nova Scotia* and do not accept that there is more than a modicum of flimsy evidence to support this theory. However, there are more and more people convinced that Sinclair's exploits were real. Books like *The Holy Blood and The Holy Grail*, which in turn foster fictional books and movies like *The Da Vinci Code*, are the ammunition for these at times fanatical beliefs. Enough people believe that Sinclair came to Nova Scotia that they erected a monument to him at Guysborough where he supposedly landed.

While waiting for the 2 p.m. starting time for our tour, we toured the small museum where there were not a lot of artifacts, but some of them very intriguing indeed. Since 2010 the new owners have found a pair of scissors that the Smithsonian has declared to be of Spanish American origin and at least 300 years old. There are fragments of low-carbon steel, brought up from deep within one of the shafts and also dated to more than 300 years, along with oak and coconut fibres from the same age. The reality certainly is that somebody had the technology to not only make a primitive steel, but the method to get it and the other organic materials down to depths of over 170 feet. Also in the museum is an old shoe found under a rotted wharf that was only discovered a few years ago. Not only is the shoe also hundreds of years old, it is the equivalent of a size 14, which would have made the wearer a giant in the days when men were much shorter on average than today. There was also an old rail car that was used to transport material from the Money Pit to a disposal site.

By far the most interesting thing in the museum is a replica of the Direction Stone that was apparently found by the original McGinnis group of explorers at a depth of over 75 feet in the Money Pit. It is an incised cypher on a type of stone not found in Nova Scotia, which has been translated to read "Forty feet below two million pounds are buried." It doesn't make a lot of sense that the persons going to all the effort of hiding the treasure would leave such a clear clue to keep on digging, and it is yet another part of the early history of the treasure hunt that is itself shrouded in mystery.

After touring the museum, we assembled out front and were divided into two groups. We were fortunate to get into the group that was led by Charles Barkhouse, a Nova Scotian who grew up in the area and who is the historian of Oak Island. He is one of the regulars on the TV show and he is also a Mason. Over the next two hours we stayed close to him and were able to get a lot of our questions answered by the one person that would know.

The tour of Oak Island is on foot via a gravel road and the total distance travelled on the tour would be about 3.2 kilometres (roughly two miles) by our estimate. People ranged from 80 to infants in strollers, so just about anyone who is ambulatory can do this tour.

The first stop was the foundation of the McGinnis homestead. After initial attempts to find the treasure were unsuccessful, the McGinnis family moved to Oak Island to set up permanent residence to make finding the treasure their full-time business. While there is nothing unusual about the stone foundation (we have seen many similar in our years of tramping around Nova Scotia), there was a very interesting artifact associated with it. What some believe to be a Portuguese marking stone lies at the back of the foundation, apparently once part of the foundation itself.

It is an unusual rock for sure, perfectly rectangular, but whether or not it is a true Portuguese marking stone remains to be verified. The one thing Charles made clear during the tour is that the current searchers do not subscribe to any one of the particular theories about Oak Island and have an absolutely open mind on the subject.

One of the more controversial theories about Oak Island is whether or not certain large boulders are situated in such a way to form various points on a very large Christian cross that covers a large part of the island. Charles pointed out a number of these during the tour, including one that had obviously been moved to sit atop a cement slab.

We came to a clearing that Charles explained had once been the lands of one Samuel Ball, who was an ex-slave from Virginia who gained his freedom by

The Money Pit, no longer a pit.

fighting for the British during the American Revolution. He was one of many free blacks who, along with thousands of other Loyalists, were evacuated from New York to Shelburne, Nova Scotia, in 1783. He made his way to Oak Island where he managed to acquire almost all of the centre of the island by purchasing lots that had been surveyed out by the Crown. Considering he left New York with only the clothes on his back, many have wondered if he found something valuable on the island to pay for those purchases. Yet another unanswered question.

Next up was South Cove, with a beautiful view of Mahone Bay with the Tancook islands in the distance.

Behind South Cove is what the searchers call 'The Swamp,' which they believe to be an artificial creation and are currently in the process of draining. They appear to be progressing quite well and, while not particularly pretty to look at, sandpipers were enjoying it.

Just up from South Cove is the site of another one of Oak Island's mysterious rock formations. Here searchers many years ago found a man-made triangle of stones, the meaning of which is contested. The original formation has long since been destroyed, but the owners have recreated it from preserved drawings. It's easier to get an idea of the formation from the sign on site than seeing it on the ground.

Some claim that it is meant to represent a sextant, and it does point in the direction of the Money Pit. To us it looked more like a sailboat. Beside the triangle is an innocent enough looking little pond, which Charles explained was once up to 90 feet deep.

Now we were getting to the serious stuff — the Money Pit. As we wrote at the beginning of this chapter, Dale had been

Borehole 10 – not the easiest place to conduct exploratory dives!

here many years ago and remembered the disappointment of finding the Money Pit to be unrecognizable as anything close to a treasure site. Not much has changed. The debris has been removed and the pit filled in — there is no pit in the Money Pit. The entire area has had the top ten feet or so of overburden removed, but it looks more like a gravel pit than a money pit.

Charles did clear up one mistaken impression we had, despite having read many books on Oak Island, namely that the Money Pit was not the place where most of the treasure seeking had been undertaken for many years. We had wrongly equated the Money Pit as the place where in 1965 four people were killed when they were overcome by noxious fumes. That site is much closer

to Smith's Cove. We also wrongly assumed it was the Money Pit down which the CBC stuck a camera in 1971 and appeared to find possible chests and a human hand. This took place at nearby Borehole 10, which is something worth seeing.

This is an amazing construction that is made up primarily of a series of oil tank rail cars that have had the ends cut off and then welded together and driven vertically into the ground. This hole goes down 140 feet and then there is another 50 feet or so of reinforced concrete until it finally ends where a large underground cavern opens up. The cavern is below the water line, so it is filled with water and apparently has a strong current at times. We cannot imagine putting on a wetsuit with an oxygen line and climbing down the ladder into the pitch black water over 200 feet from the surface and trying to find out the dimension of the opening, but that is exactly what Dan Blankenship and his son did on many occasions. Once it almost cost Dan his life as part of the borehole wall was collapsed.

Just two weeks before our visit, the searchers constructed a wooden platform from which you can peer down into the borehole and trust me, if you suffer from vertigo, this is not the place to be. There is no other spot on the island that brings home so clearly the absolute intrepidation that treasure hunters must bring to their quest.

The tour ends at Smith's Cove, which once had an artificially constructed beach that has since been replaced by more modern versions. Looking at it today, it looks like thousands of other little coves on Nova Scotia's Atlantic coastline.

The last thing Charles pointed out was a mysterious letter G inscribed in a rock at the edge of Smith's Cove, a letter associated with Freemasonry, but not being Masons he was not going to say more about it in our presence.

In truth, you probably won't be overawed by your visit to Oak Island, but you will be much better informed. Who knows, perhaps one day *The Curse of Oak Island* might finally be broken — just don't hold your breath waiting. This might not be the most scenic walk you've ever done, but trust us, it will be the most iconic. There is an aura about Oak Island that you can only experience by visiting the place. It's worth the time and patience it might take to get your reservation for a tour. And it's pretty cool to watch one of the most famous TV shows on the planet being shot right before your eyes.

Treasure-hunting detritus.

WHAT YOU NEED TO KNOW:

Name: Oak Island Tour
Address: 5 Oak Island Dr, Mahone Bay, NS B0J 2E0
Websites: facebook.com/FriendsOfOakIsland
oakislandresort.ca
history.ca/shows/the-curse-of-oak-island/
Season: Summer
Opening times: Specific tour dates
Price: $50 per ticket
Other note: Advance booking a must!
Classic photo op (Instagram worthy!): The Money Pit

7

SAIL ON *BLUENOSE II*

Bluenose II under full sail.

We have a confession to make — we have never sailed on the current version of *Bluenose*. In preparation for this book we certainly planned to sail on her, but as any Nova Scotian who has paid any attention to the news knows, the completion of what is the third version of the famed sailing ship became a boondoggle. We are not the ones who described it as such; it was our current premier Stephen McNeil who used that word in referring to a project that was supposed to have the refitted version ready to sail in 2012. It took six more years to get it right. In 2019 it spent almost the entire season outside of Nova Scotia, so few people here got to sail on it. Finally, in 2020 it will spend most of its sailing time in its home province and anyone

who wants to should be able to get aboard in Lunenburg, Halifax or a number of smaller ports where it will make an appearance.

We have sailed aboard the original *Bluenose II* a number of times and are confident that a trip around Lunenburg Harbour will be very much as it was on our last voyage there. But first, why is it such a big deal to get aboard this ship, and why in Lunenburg, as we strongly recommend?

The origin of the term 'bluenose' has a plethora of explanations and we are not going to venture a guess as to which is the correct one. However, it is indisputable that one of Thomas Chandler Haliburton's chapters in his book on Sam Slick, the Yankee clockmaker, is 'Gulling a Blue-Nose,' and establishes that the term goes back at least as far as 1838. Although Haliburton uses the term in a pejorative sense, since then Nova Scotians have adopted the sobriquet with a sense of pride that can almost certainly be traced to the fame of the sailing ship *Bluenose*. The Nova Scotia Archives describes schooners as 'the workhorses of the sea' and for hundreds of years they plied our coastal waters and made regular journeys to the Caribbean and back. A specialized version was the Grand Banks schooner, which was the ultimate in speed — a necessity for getting out to the Newfoundland fishing grounds and back as fast as possible.

William Roué, a self-taught naval architect from Halifax, designed the original *Bluenose*. It was built in the Smith & Rhuland shipyard in Lunenburg. It was not built to race; that was a by-product of its design, but it was primarily a working boat that holds the record for the largest cargo of fish ever delivered to Lunenburg by a schooner. By the time it was launched in 1921 there was already a fierce competition between Lunenburg and the Massachusetts port of Gloucester as to which could build the fastest working ship. Nova Scotia was stinging from a loss in 1920 and eager for revenge. They got it in spades. From 1921 to 1937 *Bluenose* had a record that is unsurpassed in schooner racing, although it is not true that she never lost a race.

The ship became more than just a symbol of pride for Nova Scotians, but a true Canadian icon. In 1929 she appeared on what many consider to be the most beautiful postage stamp ever produced in Canada, the 50-cent denomination of the King George V scroll issue. It shows *Bluenose* in full sail pulling away from her American rival. In 1937 she

Bluenose II's life ring lashed to the vessel's rigging.

became the symbol on the Canadian dime and has remained there ever since. Her fame was such that she was invited to the Chicago World's Fair in 1933 and to King George V's Silver Jubilee in England in 1935. Long before anyone thought of building a replica to act as Nova Scotia's sailing ambassador, the original ship was doing just that.

Some may consider the fate of the original *Bluenose* to border on tragedy. The ship was sold to a West Indian trading company, where she/it was stripped of masts and used to carry bananas before being wrecked on a reef off Haiti in 1946.

In 1963 the Oland family, whose most popular beer at the time was Schooner,

The deck of *Bluenose II*, in its home port of Lunenburg.

Captain Phil Watson joined *Bluenose II* in 1987 and was named captain in 2001.

launched *Bluenose II* as an advertising gimmick that worked out better than anticipated. Built at the same shipyard as the original, and allegedly involving some of the same people who worked on the original, she became a hit wherever she sailed. Presented as a gift to the province in 1971, it was this version of the ship that we and thousands of others have enjoyed cruises on in the harbour where she was built.

Old Town Lunenburg is a UNESCO World Heritage site founded in 1753, described by that organization as, "the best surviving example of a planned British colonial settlement in North America." It is a popular destination for tourists and needs no help from us in promoting its many attractions. The second best view of the town, with its unique architecture and colourful wooden buildings, is from the golf course on the other side of the harbour. But to get the best view you need to get on board *Bluenose II* (really *Bluenose III* or even *IV*) and take the two-hour harbour cruise. We have seen the newest version and it is a beautiful ship, and not really distinguishable from the previous version.

There is also the option of spending an entire day aboard the ship on the Deckhand for a Day program, during which *Bluenose II* sails out to the islands of Mahone Bay and back. Participants get the chance to take the helm and learn everything one needs to know about manning a Grand Banks schooner. It's not cheap, but if you want to get an in-depth *Bluenose* experience it might be just the thing.

There's likely no symbol of Nova Scotia more iconic than *Bluenose II* — it's featured on every Canadian dime after all — and a photo opportunity from her decks is a bucket list item for Nova Scotians and visitors from around the world. Add to this a visit to Old Town Lunenburg's wide selection of shops and cafés and you have an experience you will never forget. We are truly looking forward to our first trip aboard this version of Nova Scotia's most famous goodwill ambassador. Maybe we'll see you on board!

WHAT YOU NEED TO KNOW:

Name: *Bluenose II*
Address: 121 Bluenose Drive, Lunenburg, NS
Website: bluenose.novascotia.ca
whc.unesco.org/en/list/741
Season: Summer
Opening times: 2 cruises a day (a.m. and p.m.)
Price: $68 per adult
Other note: Discounted youth tickets
Classic photo op (Instagram worthy!): The *Bluenose* name on the bow

VIEW NOVA SCOTIA'S **DARK SKY** PRESERVE **TWO DIFFERENT WAYS**

The Sky Circle at Kejimkujik National Park. (Image courtesy of Parks Canada/Chris Green.)

Growing up in northern Manitoba, Dale was accustomed to seeing the aurora borealis (northern lights), the Milky Way and meteors as well as Mercury, Venus, Mars and Jupiter all visible to the naked eye. At times the starlight was so bright that you could read by it. All that disappeared from view when he moved to Winnipeg and then Halifax, lost in the ever-present glare of the artificial light that is a 24/7 reality of urban life. Sadly, most Canadians have never experienced seeing the night sky as it has looked to our ancestors for thousands of years and have no understanding of the wonder and awe it inspired in them. Fortunately, the value of preserving the view of the true night sky has been recognized in recent years and in 1999 the Royal Astronomical Society of Canada designated the first Dark Sky Preserve at Torrens Barrens in northern Ontario.

According to the society's website (RASC.ca):

A Dark-Sky Preserve is an area in which no artificial lighting is visible and active measures are in place to educate and promote the reduction of light pollution to the public and nearby municipalities. Sky glow from beyond the borders of the Preserve will be of comparable intensity, or less, to that of natural sky glow.

It is important to keep in mind the requirement that the areas adjoining the Dark Sky Preserve be equally free of light pollution.

In 2010 Kejimkujik National Park, or Keji, was designated a Dark Sky Preserve.

oTENTiks are exclusive to Canada's national parks and national historic sites. There are 10 available to rent at Jeremy's Bay campground.

It is the only one in Nova Scotia. There are myriad reasons to visit Keji, which is the only national park that is also a national historic site. Indigenous people have been traversing its waterways for thousands of years, leaving behind petroglyphs that are now protected from further destruction by vandals and curiosity seekers. The lakes and streams provide some of the best canoeing experiences in Canada and are the subject of Chapter 9. Keji is also the best place we know in Nova Scotia to teach your children the joys of fat tire cycling, with many kilometres of gentle gravel paths alongside the shores of Lake Kejimkujik, but with enough ups and downs over roots and rocks to make it exciting for kids of all ages. There

are over 100 kilometres of hiking trails, from the 0.2-kilometre, wheelchair-accessible Mersey Meadow to a multi-day wilderness hike around the perimeter of the park on the Liberty Lake trail.

Parks Canada has gone out of its way to provide a wide variety of accommodations options in the park. There are traditional campsites for tenters and RVers as well as 52 backcountry wilderness campsites, but there is also the option of staying in a yurt, a wilderness cabin or, our new favourite, an oTENTik.

Since Keji has been designated as a Dark Sky Preserve, Parks Canada has provided summer visitors with the opportunity to observe the stars, planets and constellations

The Milky Way over Eel Weir in Kejimkujik National Park. (Image courtesy of Parks Canada/Chris Green.)

from the Sky Circle, located not far from the principal campground at Jeremy's Bay.

Every Tuesday and Friday nights when the skies are clear, beginning at 9:30 or 10:00 p.m. depending on the length of daylight, a group of up to 30 can view the dark sky through a powerful telescope placed in the Sky Circle. The 90-minute program includes a combination of astronomical facts and legends and myths inspired by the stars and planets. Twice a year Keji holds Dark Sky Weekends, which feature a much more in-depth experience for those interested in more than the Sky Circle observatory.

One amenity that greatly enhances the night sky experience is renting a Dark Sky Kit from the Interpretive Centre near the park entrance. For $5 you get the use of a pair of Celestron 8x42 mm binoculars, a red light headlamp, a star finder and other material designed to make it easier to identify stars, planets and constellations.

Every Wednesday night there is an opportunity to travel under the night sky by bicycle. Guides lead up to a dozen riders on a two-hour tour after dark using red headlamps, which are preferable to white lights for dark-sky viewing. There is a fee of $14.70 for these rides, and if you don't have a bike you can rent one at Jake's Landing within the park.

Reservations for most of these programs can be made on the Parks Canada website at pc.gc.ca/en/pn-np/ns/kejimkujik.

What if you would like to experience the Dark Sky Preserve, but aren't up for camping or even an oTENTik? There is a great alternative that is about as far removed from roughing it as one could imagine, but still provides the opportunity to view the night sky through a variety of telescopes with a trained astronomy expert.

Trout Point Lodge is unlike any other resort in Nova Scotia and must be seen to

Trout Point Lodge, on the banks of the Tusket River in a remote part of southwest Nova Scotia, an ideal location for stargazing.

be believed. A luxury resort, it is two hours southwest of Keji or a three-hour drive from Halifax, deep within the massive 1.5 million hectare UNESCO Southwest Nova Biosphere Reserve. The location is remote: Trout Point Lodge was built at the end of a narrow 3-kilometre-long dirt road that is itself off another dirt road that branches off Highway 203 — the most remote paved road in Nova Scotia.

In the late 1990s Vaughn Perret and Charles Leary, natives of Louisiana, purchased a large tract of wilderness land on the edge of the Tobeatic Wilderness Area, which, like Keji, lies entirely within the Southwest Nova Biosphere. Picking a location on the banks of

the Tusket River, their intent was to build a lodge and outbuildings in the style of grand late-19th-century and early-20th-century wooden lodges in national and state parks throughout the United States. Using huge eastern spruce sustainably harvested in New Brunswick and native granite and sandstone they succeeded beyond anyone's expectations.

In addition to the wooden and stone exterior, almost all the furniture in the lodge was made from scratch by local artisans using local materials. For example, each of the eight bedrooms in the main lodge features custom-made wood bed frames that add an air of authenticity to the rustic but luxurious nature of Trout Point.

Kayaking on the Tusket River, close to Trout Point Lodge, in the Southwest Nova Scotia Biosphere Reserve.

The lodge opened in 2000 and after a few lean years started to gain worldwide recognition for the unique experiences available at the lodge and the surrounding area. These include some expected activities, such as canoeing or kayaking the Tusket River, hiking (the trail to Billy's Hill, the highest point in Southwest Nova Scotia, is a must-do), fly fishing and mountain biking. Other activities that one might not expect include Japanese-style forest bathing, foraging for wild mushrooms and other edibles, relaxing in a wood-fired hot tub overlooking the river, having a spa treatment while gazing at the primeval forest or joining a cooking class.

Trout Point is noted for a number of firsts, including being the first in Canada to have its kitchen certified as sustainable by the Sustainable Restaurant Association, a British-based organization whose standards on sustainability are the equivalent of Michelin. The quality of the cuisine at Trout Point, prepared by European-trained chefs with

credentials from some of the best restaurants in the world, is as good as you will get in Nova Scotia. The emphasis is almost exclusively on locally grown, foraged or caught seafood, game, vegetables, nuts and berries.

Each morning starts off with a wonderful breakfast buffet. Picnic lunches are available for expeditions on the river or in the woods. Dinner features a cocktail hour followed by a four-course meal with a huge selection of local and imported wines.

Trout Point has another first, this time in the world. In 2014 it became the first in the world to be certified as a Starlight Hotel by the Starlight Foundation, an arm of UNESCO aimed at preserving dark skies throughout the world and identifying places where observation of the true night sky can be undertaken.

Trout Point has an array of telescopes and binoculars, which on clear nights are transported to an elevated viewing platform where trained astronomers will help identify up to seven planets and many of their moons,

Telescopes and stargazers at Trout Point Lodge.

all the brightest stars, various constellations, distant galaxies and nearby satellites. One of the very best times to visit is during the annual Perseid meteor showers that occur in mid-August. If it's not a year with a full moon, you can expect to see up to 200 meteors an hour. In 2017 we visited Trout Point during the Perseids and had an experience unlike anything we have had before or after when it comes to stargazing. Not only were there dozens and dozens of meteors, there was also a fireball, which is a meteor so close that you can hear the sound of it burning as it enters Earth's atmosphere.

In 2018 Trout Point was purchased by Patrick and Pamela Wallace and they have maintained the high standards set by Charles and Vaughn from the day it opened. If we make this place sound almost too good to be true, it is because we love coming here and over the course of many visits have never failed to be impressed by the quality of the food, the hospitality and the many, many activities one can participate in, most notably the stargazing.

Trout Point is the only member in Canada of the prestigious Small Luxury Hotels of the World organization. It is a luxury hotel and the prices are correspondingly high. However, we think everyone, Nova Scotian and visitors alike, should make the splurge to stay here at least once. You won't regret it.

Viewing the night sky as it was seen by our ancestors for hundreds of thousands of years is an experience that makes a direct connection to earlier times, something not easy to do in this busy, mostly urban world. The fact that we have a Dark Sky Preserve in Nova Scotia is marvel enough, but being able to experience it in two totally different ways is something that we believe might be unique in all of Canada.

USEFUL WEBSITES:

pc.gc.ca/en/pn-np/ns/kejimkujik
troutpoint.com
rasc.ca
whynotadventure.ca
astronomynovascotia.ca

PADDLE THE **TOBEATIC WILDERNESS AREA**

A cairn at the mouth of the Beaverskin River.

People have been paddling the rivers and lakes of Nova Scotia almost since the last Ice Age. Long before there were any roads or railways, rivers were the preferred method of moving about and provided reliable passage from one coast to another. Perhaps the greatest engineering project ever undertaken in Nova Scotia was the Shubenacadie Canal that connected Halifax Harbour to the Bay of Fundy. Beginning in 1826, it took 35 years to complete and only operated for a decade, but it has become a symbol of an era when travel by water was an essential part of everyday life in Nova Scotia. Thankfully the Shubenacadie Canal Commission is tasked with preserving as much of the canal as possible and recently completed a partial restoration of the marine railway in Dartmouth that marked the eastern end of the canal. It is well worth walking the pathway from the Dartmouth waterfront to Sullivan's Pond, which follows the route of the old railway that transported boats on their final journey to the harbour.

You can still paddle across Nova Scotia using the same route as the canal. An extended canoe trip, for those with the ability and skill, is a wonderful way to fully experience nature and get away from civilization, even if only for a few days. Very few people get to have this kind of true wilderness experience; one that involves no organized campground, no electricity, no washroom facilities, no cell service and probably no people other than the ones you are travelling with. We are

TOBEACTIC
WILDERNESS AREA
(shaded in yellow)

Amherst

Pictou

Annapolis Royal
Kentville

Truro

Sydney

Digby

Windsor

Yarmouth

Lunenburg

Halifax/Dartmouth

Liverpool

Shelburne

fortunate that we have a group of friends who are expert canoeists with outdoor skills and have travelled with them on a number of occasions to some of the remotest parts of Nova Scotia. There are still places in this province that it takes two or three days by canoe to reach.

Despite its small size, Nova Scotia offers a number of extended canoe routes. Canoe Kayak Nova Scotia, the province's recreational paddling organization, identifies 94 canoe routes in all regions of the province, of which at least a third offer the chance for a multi-day trip. There are some that involve few, if any, portages, such as the Annapolis and upper Musquodoboit rivers, but depending on the water level most involve some portaging. In our opinion, by far the best place to get the

The endangered Blanding's Turtle, found in isolated populations in southwestern Nova Scotia.

Dale with his Tent Dweller's ceremonial paddle.

wilderness experience is somewhere in the vast Southwest Nova Biosphere Reserve. Recognized by UNESCO as one of Earth's unique ecosystems, it covers an astounding 1.5 million hectares that encompasses virtually all of southwest Nova Scotia's five counties. It includes Kejimkujik National Park, the Tobeatic Wilderness Area (the largest in the Maritimes) and the Shelburne River Wilderness Area. Nine significant rivers flow from the interior of the Tobeatic to the Atlantic and Bay of Fundy, each of which provides a challenge for all but the most advanced paddlers. However, there are routes that are less strenuous and still get as far away from 21st century life as one can in Nova Scotia. One of these is the fabled Tent Dwellers' route.

In 1908 Albert Bigelow Paine published *The Tent Dwellers*, which described a journey into the interior of the Tobeatic and has become a classic of outdoor literature. Combining humour and wit, Paine described a series of travails that individually sounded awful, but collectively amounted to an adventure of a lifetime. In 2008, to mark the centenary of the book, Parks Canada sponsored a recreation of the Tent Dwellers' trip and Dale was fortunate to be one of the eight people asked to participate. It was a planned seven-day trip that got extended to eight because of bad weather, but like the original trip it was the ultimate Nova Scotia wilderness experience.

This is an example of the type of terrain that you will encounter while paddling the

Shelburne River, which is a major part of the Tent Dwellers' route. There is the very real possibility of seeing moose, black bear or even a bobcat in this area, along with dozens of species of woodland birds seldom encountered anywhere near a town or city. Rocks like those in the photo on the opposite page often have snapping or painted turtles sunning themselves on them. There is also the chance of spotting the extremely rare Blanding's turtle, which, east of Quebec, is only found in small pockets of southwest Nova Scotia. There are estimated to be less than 200 in the province. You can find a number of species of frogs in the area and if you visit in spring when the water is highest and before the blackflies come out, you might be serenaded by hundreds of spring peepers. If you miss the peepers, you will almost certainly hear the quack-like sounds of the wood frog.

It's not just what's above the water that is interesting. While brook trout are under siege by invasive species like small-mouthed bass and chain pickerel in much of Nova Scotia, there is still a decent native population in many parts of the Tobeatic. During the Tent Dwellers trip, we had a number of meals of freshly caught trout, so bring your fishing rod and licence.

In addition to the animal denizens of the Tobeatic, there are a great variety of flowers and shrubs that you won't find in your backyard. Rhodora is the hardiest member of the azalea family and from May to June puts out a wonderful pink blossom that covers hundreds of acres of the wetlands that abound in the area. It is a sight worth paddling a good distance to see. Sporting Lake Nature Reserve comprises three islands in Sporting Lake that have never been

Rhodora, in bloom.

touched by humankind. Here you can land your canoe and walk amidst forest giants — hemlock, white pine and red spruce. This is one of the best remaining examples of an Acadian climax forest anywhere. It's not easy to get to, which explains why it avoided the loggers, but like the rhodora shrubbery well worth the effort.

The fact that there are so few old-growth trees left, even in this wilderness area, attests to the presence of humans here in numbers much greater than today, for both profit and pleasure. There are a number of human-made flumes that were once used to float logs down into rivers and on to sawmills that once dotted every part of southwest Nova Scotia. Coming across one miles from the nearest road reminds us that humans and their enterprises come and go, but that nature will, when left alone, always rejuvenate.

At the outflow of the Shelburne River into Lake Rossignol there is an old abandoned boat that allegedly belonged to famed writer

Dale and Sherman Embree at Bat's Rest on Little Tobeatic Lake.

of western tales Zane Grey, who caught a world record bluefin tuna out of Liverpool in 1924. How it got here is a mystery and an illustration of the type of things you might come across while paddling in the Tobeatic. At one time there were a series of ranger cabins, each a day's paddle apart, that formed a circular route for game wardens to patrol what was then the Tobeatic Game Sanctuary. Most of these are long gone, but a few remain, such Bat's Rest on Little Tobeatic Lake. As the name suggests, it was the home of many bats before white-nose syndrome wiped most of them out. The cabin is currently being restored by a group of volunteers.

While the Tent Dwellers' route has become very popular, it has some very long portages and is grueling at times. There are other routes starting in Kejimkujik that offer multi-day opportunities for less experienced paddlers. Foremost among these is the Big Dam/Frozen Ocean route, which provides the perfect three-day getaway on a circular route. It starts at the Big Dam Lake parking lot, from where you'll need to carry your canoe and supplies 400 metres to the lake. From here it proceeds through Big Dam Lake and an 800-metre portage to Still Brook, where the reward is a wonderful paddle down into Frozen Ocean Lake. The route has numerous small camping spots, which you very well might have to make use of. The next day there are some rapids that can be run at high water or portaged around at low, but overall this is a relaxing day of paddling down mostly still water to Channel Lake and a campground at the beginning and end of the last portage, which is also 800

Shelburne River, below Irving Lake.

metres but can be avoided in high water by good canoeists. On the third day it's down the Little River into Kejumkujik Lake and along the shoreline to the landing point at Jim Charles Point.

This trip is offered as a guided tour by Whynot Adventure, who are Kejimkujik specialists and will provide a safe and enjoyable way to introduce you and your family to the joy of paddling.

As we get older, we regret that we did not spend more time in a canoe exploring all nine of those rivers that flow out of the Tobeatic. We have friends who have traversed them all and while some of their stories are pretty hairy, none of them ever regretted spending time on the rivers of the deep woods.

Paddling down a gently flowing stream or on a calm lake is one of the most enjoyable and relaxing ways we know of to de-stress and get away from it all. The sound of the paddle slicing the water has a calming effect that has become an integral part of the Canadian ethos. On the other hand, the adrenalin rush from taking on a set of rapids at the limit of your paddling ability is almost unequalled in a recreational activity in Nova Scotia. Whether you are paddling to calm your nerves or to set them on edge, getting out on one of our legendary water routes is a must for everyone looking for some outdoor adventure.

USEFUL WEBSITES:

ckns.ca
pc.gc.ca
novascotia.ca/nse/protectedareas/
wa_tobeatic.asp
swnovabiosphere.ca
whynotadventure.ca

10

DISCOVER THE **HISTORY OF THE LOYALISTS**

Cox's Historic Shipyard and Warehouse.

The town of Shelburne has less than 1,800 residents, but over 230 years ago it was, for a brief time, the fourth largest city in North America with over 17,000 refugees from the newly independent United States of America. Nearby was Birchtown, the largest community of freed black slaves in the world. The story of the United Empire Loyalists, black and white, is one of the most compelling narratives in all Nova Scotian history and warrants a visit to both places, situated on the third largest natural harbour on the planet.

Not everyone who lived in the Thirteen Colonies was happy about the Americans' victory in the revolution that started in 1775 and ended with British recognition of independence in 1783. These people were generally referred to as Loyalists by the British and traitors by the Americans. New York City, which remained in British hands for the entirety of the conflict, was a hotbed of Loyalist sentiment, and by the time the Treaty of Paris was signed in 1783 over 50,000 refugees were ready to be transported to new homes somewhere in Canada. Of these, 30,000 ended up in the British colony of Nova Scotia, which at that time also included New Brunswick.

During the revolution, many black slaves were promised their freedom if they fought for the Crown. Although most of the 100,000 slaves who crossed over to British lines were left behind, over 2,500 did make

it to the Shelburne area, where they settled in a community named for British General Samuel Birch, who signed their Certificates of Freedom.

Visiting Shelburne and Birchtown today involves two dramatically different settings that need to be experienced in tandem to get a clear idea of what both sets of refugees endured in seeking freedom in a new land.

The town of Shelburne has a dramatic location on Shelburne Harbour that includes Dock Street, probably the best-preserved historic district in Nova Scotia. Within a ten-block radius there are many well-preserved homes and businesses that date from the late 1700s, and the Shelburne Museum Complex that features one of only two remaining dory shops in Canada — the other is in Lunenburg. Dories are the iconic small fishing boats that were carried aboard Grand Banks schooners and lowered into

the water where a two-person crew would jig for cod and halibut until the boat was full. Rowing a dory is great exercise and you can still order a custom-made dory from the J.C. Williams Dory Shop today.

Part of the museum complex is Cox's Warehouse, seen above along with the Dory Shop, and the Ross-Thomson House, which dates from 1785 and doubled as a home and store for early Shelburne merchant brothers George and Robert Ross. Many thousands of Canadians trace their roots back to the Loyalists and the Shelburne County Museum has a great collection of genealogical material that is available to the public, as well as exhibits reflecting the multi-cultural nature of the people of this area, from the Mi'kmaq to the Acadians to the Loyalists, and even the oldest Welsh settlement in Canada.

The well-preserved historic look of Shelburne's waterfront didn't happen by

The Cooper's Inn, built in 1784.

accident. In the 1990s Hollywood came to town and used the waterfront as the background setting for a number of movies, most notably *The Scarlet Letter* and *Moby Dick*. In order to give an even more authentic 17th and 18th century look, all power lines and cables were buried, a steeple was added to Cox's Warehouse and several new buildings were erected to look as if they were hundreds of years old. Movies and television series are still shot here on a regular basis.

In order to appreciate the Shelburne experience, we recommend spending a night or two at the Cooper's Inn B&B, one of the original grand homes on the waterfront that dates from 1784. It was built by a blind Loyalist from Boston, George Gracie, who became a prominent figure in early Nova Scotian politics. It offers packages that include admission to both the Shelburne museums and the Black Loyalist Heritage Centre as well as a meal at the award-winning Charlotte Lane Café where Chef Roland Glauser has been serving up the best of Nova Scotia from land and sea for three decades.

Not everything that went on in the early days of Shelburne was sweetness and light. The soil in southwest Nova Scotia is not much good for growing anything more than root vegetables, so although there were hundreds of land grants parcelled out, most of them could not sustain a family. The majority of the people who arrived from the United States eventually moved on, but before doing so Shelburne had the dubious distinction of being home to the first race riot in North America. Not only had free blacks

An exhibit in the Black Loyalist Heritage Centre. African masks traditionally represented the spirit of the ancestors.

come to Nova Scotia, but white Loyalists are estimated to have brought as many as 1,200 slaves with them, a fact that seems almost incomprehensible today. The free blacks were not given land grants equal in size or fertility, such as it was, as the white Loyalists. As a result, many of them offered their services as indentured servants or worked for wages well below what a white labourer would expect. Tensions ran high, and in 1784 a mob of whites attacked and demolished the home of black Baptist preacher David George. Ten days of rioting followed, during which most of the free blacks who had tried to establish themselves in Shelburne were forced to relocate to Birchtown. The two settlements remained racially divided for centuries.

With this background in mind, it is time to visit the Black Loyalist Heritage Centre, which takes up the story from the viewpoint of the free black Loyalists.

Today Birchtown is suffering the same fate as many other small rural communities in Nova Scotia — depopulation. The one-room schoolhouse closed in 1960 and on a recent visit we were told that descendants of only six of the many original families who came to Birchtown still live there. However, Birchtown has something other dying communities do not, a beacon of hope in the Black Loyalist Heritage Centre, which opened in 2015 and now draws visitors from around the world.

There is an incredible irony about how this place got built, as it stemmed from yet another race-based crime. In 2006 the Black Loyalist Society's main office, which stood on this spot and contained thousands of important records, photos and other archival material, was burnt to the ground by an arsonist who has never been caught. The act so galvanized and embarrassed the people

Archaeologists discovered the remains of pit houses in the mid 1990s. Here Dale is outside a reconstructed pit house.

of Nova Scotia that the money required to build this new and much larger structure was raised in a very short period of time. One cannot but be struck by the modernity and technological advancement of this property and the contrast with centuries-old buildings in Shelburne, proving that there is more than one way to present the story of an important part of Canadian history.

Visiting the Black Loyalist Heritage Centre involves not only the modern building, but also the one-room schoolhouse, St. Paul's Church, the site of the Black Burial Grounds on the shores of Shelburne Harbour and walking the short Heritage Trail that connects them all. One of the most arresting sites is a reconstructed pit house, which is a hole in the ground with logs overhead. Entire families, waiting for land grants that might never come, built these tiny homes. Compare that to the grand houses of some of the white Loyalists only kilometres away across the harbour.

The Black Loyalist Heritage Centre is not limited to telling the story of Birchtown, but rather all of the communities where free black Loyalists settled after the revolution. This map on the Shaw Turret shows those settlements in a setting that gives a fine view of the church, burial ground and Birchtown shoreline.

Inside, the huge Lindsay Gallery uses a combination of multimedia and artifacts to tell the story of the black Loyalists, starting with their capture in Africa, their transport and enslavement in the United States, their journey and reception in Nova Scotia and finally a chapter of the history few Nova Scotians are aware of — their return to Africa. For some, conditions in Nova Scotia were not much better than the slavery they endured in the United States. In 1791 a group of black Loyalists petitioned the king to allow them to return to Africa, in particular the colony of Sierra Leone and the city of Freetown. The request was granted and in 1792 over one third of the black Loyalists, including the preacher David George whose house had been destroyed in the 1784 race riots, left for Africa. Since the centre opened in 2015, some descendants of those who left Nova Scotia have returned from Sierra Leone to visit. Theirs is a compelling story of which Nova Scotia played a significant part, one that we certainly cannot take any pride in.

On paying the admission fee to the centre you will be given a small business card with the name and face of a black Loyalist on it. You can follow that person's journey through the various stages of their life by looking them up at each station of the chronological wall. The screens in the photo above are touch-activated and each provides great detail on all aspects of the African diaspora, of which the black Loyalists were a part.

On display is a digital replica of the Book of Negroes, which was a record kept by the British navy of every black Loyalist who came to Nova Scotia. It provided the inspiration for Lawrence Hill's best-selling novel of the same name. One of the most interesting things to do at the Black Loyalist Heritage Centre is to create your own digital quilt using pieces similar to those used to make the Black Loyalist Journey quilt, which is on display. It shows the four stages of the journey from Africa to the United States to Nova Scotia and finally back to Africa.

A whirligig, a hand-crafted wind machine.

We believe every Nova Scotian and visitor to the province should visit Shelburne and Birchtown to get the complete story of the Loyalists. If you can, time your trip with the Shelburne Kayak Festival in August or the Whirligig Festival (brightly coloured and often ingenious pieces of folk art) in September, when the weather is usually perfect.

WHAT YOU NEED TO KNOW:

Name: Black Loyalist Heritage Centre
Address: 119 Old Birchtown Road, Shelburne, NS B0T 1W0
Websites: blackloyalist.novascotia.ca whirligigfestival.com shelburnekayakfestival.ca
Season: Year-round
Opening times: Most days 10-5pm
Price: <$10
Other note: Enjoy a guided tour

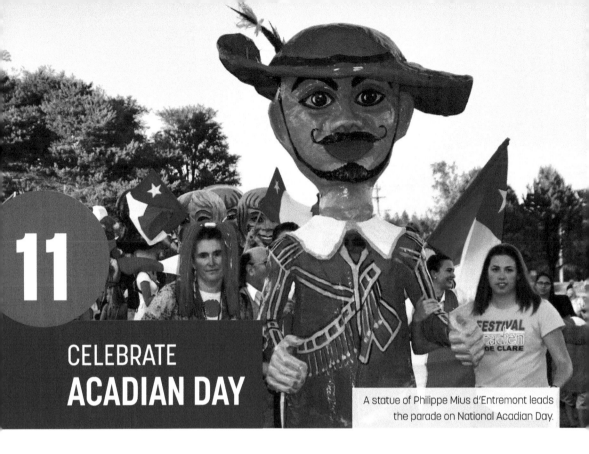

11

CELEBRATE
ACADIAN DAY

A statue of Philippe Mius d'Entremont leads
the parade on National Acadian Day.

On August 15 every year, major celebrations take place in Acadian communities throughout the Maritimes. Years ago, we were visiting friends in the tiny village of Petit-Rocher, New Brunswick, without any idea that we were there on Acadian Day. Suddenly the only street in the place was flooded with people decked out in the red, white, blue and yellow of the Acadian flag, marching together and banging on pots, drums and anything that would make a racket, while singing and laughing at the same time. We'd never seen anything like it. Our New Brunswick friends, most of whom are Acadians, told us that we were witnessing a tintamarre, which translates as making a din or clamour. It comes from the same root as Tantramar, the name

given to the large marsh on the Chignecto Isthmus that separates New Brunswick and Nova Scotia because of the loud cries of the thousands of ducks and geese the Acadians found there in the 17th and 18th centuries. We were fascinated by this unexpected cultural event, and with a little research found that anyone could join in the celebrations in numerous places in Nova Scotia. It is one of the most fun things you can do in Nova Scotia and everyone should attend and participate in at least one tintamarre in their lifetime. We'll explain how to participate, but first a little more on the Acadians.

Who exactly are the Acadians and how did they get that name? The answers are not simple. In 1524 Italian explorer Giovanni da Verrazzano, sailing for France, made the first of a number of voyages to the New World. On the first voyage he mapped the area from roughly North Carolina north to Cape Cod. He was the first to enter present day New York Harbor and the bridge that now straddles its entrance is named for him. He certainly sailed very close to Nova Scotia on his return voyage to France, but it is unlikely he ever set foot in the area we now call Acadia. Instead, on a map he named the region around present day Virginia 'Arcadia,' a reference to an area of ancient Greece known for its idyllic landscape. Arcadian is still used to describe a simple, quiet rural place or way of life.

Between Verrazzano's voyage and Samuel de Champlain's in 1604 to the coasts of Nova Scotia, New Brunswick and Maine, map makers had somehow transported Arcadia over 1,000 miles north to a region that included northern Maine, the Maritime Provinces and even a portion of eastern Quebec. Along the way the letter 'r' was dropped, and the place was referred to as La Cadie by the French and Acadia by the English. The name was in place before a single French settler ever set foot in the region.

The background of the Acadians is significantly different from those who settled the area that became known as Quebec and its inhabitants, Quebecois or French Canadians. The latter group springs from about 8,500 immigrants, almost all from northwest France, who arrived over a 150-year period between the founding of Quebec City in 1608 to the fall of that city to the British in 1759. The Acadians come from a much smaller stock of immigrants that started arriving in the Annapolis Valley in the 1620s from the district of Vienne, a department in west central France that, surprisingly, does not border the ocean, given the Acadians well-known proclivity for draining marshlands by way of dykes.

The first child born in Acadia was Mathieu Martin, who arrived in 1636 at Port-Royal, the settlement founded by Champlain in 1605. Later, Acadian settlements were founded in various parts of Nova Scotia, New Brunswick and Prince Edward Island as well as Maine. However, the period of French immigration to most of Acadia was effectively curtailed after the English were ceded control of mainland Nova Scotia by the Treaty of Utrecht in 1713.

The story of the expulsion of the Acadians is well known, and documented further in Chapter 15. The question we've been asked a number of times by visitors is, "If the Acadians were expelled, why are they still here?" While many Acadians fled to the woods and managed to avoid deportation until the war was over, the greater number of Acadians were those who were allowed to return from where they had been sent, mostly New England, after 1763. The catch was that they could not return to the rich farmlands of the Annapolis Valley, which were being granted to a group known as the New England Planters. Nor could they settle in one region to create a large Catholic presence. This resulted in the creation of a number of new Acadian settlements in places as disparate as Cheticamp on Cape Breton Island and Chezzetcook on the Eastern Shore.

We do not want to give the impression that anywhere near the number of Acadians who were expelled returned. Our research puts the number at no more than 1,600 and

The universally recognized symbol of the Acadian nation is the flag, featuring the Stella Maris in the blue stripe.

there are far more Acadian descendants in Quebec, Maine and most notably Louisiana where they identify as Cajuns, which comes from the word Acadian. The Acadian expulsion was a true diaspora that left very few of the original people in their ancestral home. They are survivors in every sense of the word and have, over the last 250-plus years, created a distinct cultural identity that is quite rightly celebrated.

National Acadian Day dates back to a conference held in Memramcook, New Brunswick, in 1881 when August 15, Assumption Day (the day the Virgin Mary ascended to heaven), was chosen over the other contender, June 24, St. Jean Baptiste Day, which is the national day of the French Canadians. Mary is the patron saint of Acadia and the decision makers wanted to emphasize that Acadians were quite distinct from their Quebec brethren. Today it is celebrated in a number of communities around the province,

but the largest gatherings are at the Le Village Historique Acadien de la Nouvelle-Écosse in Pubnico and the amazing 35-kilometre tintamarre parade in the District of Clare. It is possible to attend both celebrations on the same day, as we did recently.

Pubnico has roots in the Indigenous word Pogomcoup or Pogomkook, which has varying translations, all completely different, so we won't try to guess which one is accurate. This is the oldest continuously settled Acadian community in Nova Scotia, save for a quite brief period when the inhabitants were deported to New England. The wooden statue on page 77 is of Philippe Mius d'Entremont, who founded the community in 1653. There are hundreds of Muis(e) and d'Entremont families in the area that trace their roots back to this one man, who was a real baron.

The modern building behind Phillipe is the entrance to the Le Village Historique

The visitor centre of the Historic Acadian Village, on a beautiful 17-acre site.

Acadien de la Nouvelle-Écosse, which opened in 1999 on a 17-acre site overlooking the salt marshes and islands of West Pubnico harbour. We believe it has one of the most beautiful locations of any of the Nova Scotia provincial museums.

If you come here on Acadian Day the entrance fee is waived. You should try to arrive around 11 a.m. to make sure you get a chance to sample the fricot, a traditional Acadian stew with chicken, vegetables and dumplings that is offered by the museum's Café du Crique. It sells out fast, but there are other great offerings available, including delicious lobster sandwiches and sugar pie for dessert.

The first thing you will notice on entering any Acadian district in Nova Scotia is the abundance of the red, white and blue flag with the yellow star (Stella Maris) in the blue

stripe. The Acadian flag was officially adopted in 1884, and, if there is one universally recognized symbol of the Acadian nation, it is this flag. Not surprisingly, on Acadian Day this flag is draped on almost every building and many Acadians are wearing some version of these colours.

The museum grounds contain a number of buildings that were transplanted here from nearby communities to create the setting much as it would have existed around the beginning of the 20th century, although many of buildings are much older. The emphasis is on fishing and farming, which were and still are the mainstays of this region for hundreds of years.

You'll find a working blacksmith forge, a large shed for building dories, several intact homes where you might find the women

The view over the Pubnico Harbour from the Acadian Village.

Dale and Alison at the tintamarre.

cooking rappie pie over a wooden stove or working on a quilt or someone who can demonstrate how fishers made their own nets. From the wharf you can view *La Tatane*, a reproduction of a typical Pubnico lobster boat from around 1900. With its single sail and open hull, it is a far cry from the massive lobster boats that are now built in Pubnico to fish the richest lobster grounds in the world.

In addition to touring the museum grounds, on Acadian Day you can listen to live musicians playing traditional songs of the region, have your own picnic or share the *Bon Ami* that surrounds the entire day. What if you don't speak French? Will you feel like an outsider? Absolutely not. The Acadians are about the most welcoming people we've ever come across and you'll hear as much English spoken as French. We saw licence plates from a dozen provinces and states, including Louisiana.

Young dancers in the parade in Clare.

From Pubnico it's an easy drive to the Clare district on the shores of the Bay of Fundy, where the tintamarre will start at the tiny village of Salmon River at 6:00 p.m. and make its way to the campus of the Université Sainte-Anne almost 35 kilometres away. If you are going to see and participate in this tintamarre, we strongly suggest staying somewhere along the route. You can watch as the decorated cars go by and then join the end of the parade in your own vehicle. In our opinion, the best choice is the Au Havre du Capitaine in Meteghan River, where owner/manager Louise Comeau will not only give you a warm welcome but provide the items you need to participate in the tintamarre. That was how we were decked out on our last visit.

The spectators stand on the side of the highway and as the first vehicles approach the noise gets deafening, both from the sirens and honking of horns, but also from the banging of pots and pans and other noise makers by those cheering them on.

After the last vehicle in the parade passed by, we hopped in our car and joined the parade. Neither of us had ever been in a parade before and it was both strange and quite exhilarating to be cheered on by people waving flags and making noise.

It was surprisingly easy to find a parking space at the university grounds and then take in the Grande Marche, which is a pedestrian parade led by none other than Philippe Mius d'Entremont.

After the parade there's more live music, food and fun. There's a reason the term *joie de vivre* is French and if you ever thought the Acadians were a people who dwell on their past, then a visit on Acadian Day will completely dispel that notion. It's a day you'll never forget.

USEFUL WEBSITES:

levillage.novascota.ca
havreducapitaine.ca
museeacadien.ca

12

DISCOVER **DIGBY NECK**
AND ITS ISLANDS

Lobster boats at the
wharf in Westport.

When we were travelling to every part of Nova Scotia in the mid-1990s to garner information for the first edition of *Exploring Nova Scotia*, there was no area of our province that pleasantly surprised us more than Digby Neck and the two islands off its tip. Not only was there great natural beauty, some unique history, two great ferry crossings and two of the most interesting little villages in Nova Scotia, but whale watching like we had never experienced anywhere before or since. We have returned a number of times since that first visit and it always feels as exciting as the first time. Every Nova Scotian and visitor to the province should make a pilgrimage to this most interesting part of the province.

If you look at the upper left-hand side of any map of Nova Scotia, you will see what looks like a narrow strip of land jutting out into the Bay of Fundy near where it meets the Gulf of Maine — this is Digby Neck. At the end of it lie two islands in a row. The first and longer one is Long Island and the smaller one at the very end is Brier Island. Collectively, the three almost exactly resemble a human finger. Geologically, this is an extension of the North Mountain of the Annapolis Valley, broken into three parts, and is composed of the same basaltic rock that makes up most of that volcanic ridge. Basalt is known for forming into interlocking hexagonal blocks, most famously at Giant's Causeway in Northern

Ireland. The same type of formations are found in many places along the shores of the Bay of Fundy, many of which are along Digby Neck and on Brier Island.

Basalt might be interesting to look at and walk on, but it also creates a landscape that's not much good for farming and the trees that grow on it are stumpy and sparse. Thus, it's not surprising that the few people who live in this area have always made their living from the sea. In fact, pretty well everything a tourist will do while visiting this area will take place either on the shore or on the water.

There is only one way in and out of Digby Neck by land and that is Highway 217, which starts right in the town of Digby and ends when you board the ferry to Brier Island. It is paved the entire way, but we've noticed in recent years that it has not been maintained as well as it could be, and you need to keep an eye out for potholes. With that in mind let's head out from Digby and begin exploring Digby Neck.

The first stop is at Gulliver's Cove, a tiny fishing hamlet that was apparently named for a pirate, although we've never been able to find out if this is true or just a legend. It is four kilometres down a paved road that turns off from Highway 217 at Rossway. The attraction here is the 800-metre Gulliver's Cove High Cliffs trail that leads to a fantastic view over the Bay of Fundy. It's a relatively new trail and the Gulliver's Cove Trails Association is working on two more that will lead to even more spectacular views. The 1.2 kilometre Gulliver's Head trail should be open in 2020.

Returning to Highway 217 and continuing down Digby Neck will take you to one of the most scenic and interesting villages in Nova Scotia, Sandy Cove. Calling it a village is a stretch, as there are less than 70 permanent residents. As the highway leads down to the shore on the St. Marys Bay side of the peninsula you see an almost completely circular cove with a very narrow opening. There is no other cove like it in Nova Scotia that we are aware of. This is East Sandy Cove and it definitely beckons one to get out and walk to get a better idea of just how unusual and beautiful it is. However, this is not the main attraction in this area.

Just a kilometre or so away, on the Bay of Fundy side, you will find the 'real' Sandy Cove, a rare beach on a coastline that is more known for its forbidding cliffs than its protected inlets. This place is the site of one of the great mysteries of Nova Scotia, right up there with Oak Island and the *Mary Celeste*. In August 1863 a young man was found abandoned on the shore here, not necessarily an unusual event. The thing was that this fellow had had both his legs professionally amputated and bandaged and had been left with a small supply of food and water. Not only did he not speak English, but he hardly spoke at all. Who would have been so cruel as to have left this castaway in this deserted spot? To this day the answer to that question remains unresolved.

What is known is that the young man was given the name Jerome, eventually placed in an Acadian community on the other side of St. Marys Bay, provided with a $2 a week stipend by the government of Nova Scotia and lived almost 50 years without ever disclosing how or why his legs were amputated or who put him ashore at Sandy Cove. You can visit his grave in the Stella Maris Cemetery in Meteghan, marked 'Jerome.' There are many theories and we've provided a link to a more complete version

The Boars Head Lighthouse near Tiverton, a classic example of a square, tapered, wooden tower.

of them written by our friend Dr. George Burden, who often writes on medical-based mysteries: lifeasahuman.com/2011/arts-culture/history/the-story-of-jerome.

While it is nigh on impossible to get one of the spots on a tour of Oak Island, anyone can come to Sandy Cove and imagine the scene that greeted the young boy who first spotted Jerome here over 150 years ago.

Digby Neck ends at Petit Passage, which divides it from Long Island and is where you take the ferry across to the community of Tiverton. The tides in the Bay of Fundy are the highest in the world and when they are rising or falling they create an incredible current through both Petit Passage here and Grand Passage between Long Island and Brier Island. If you happen to be on the ferry when that is happening it may seem like the little boat is going to be washed out to sea. It's an eerie feeling and a bit scary, but it is also a demonstration of the power of the tides that you can only get on these two ferry rides.

Crossing to the village of Tiverton, keep an eye out for the Boars Head Lighthouse on the Bay of Fundy side of Petit Passage. Depending if the gate is open or not you can drive or hike up to the lighthouse, which has protected status and is considered one of the best examples of a pepper-shaker design in Nova Scotia.

About five minutes further on Highway 217 is one of the must-see attractions on the Fundy coast and it's free. Balancing Rock is an almost impossible to believe nine-metre-tall column of basalt that looks as if you could push it over with a finger. You can't. In fact, when bored fishermen put a rope around it and tried to pull it down with their boat it didn't budge.

Years ago, when we first visited Balancing Rock, there was only a narrow path through the woods and when you reached the area where the land starts to fall away you had to slide on your back in places to avoid going over the cliff. However, it was worth it because at that time you could stand and get your photo taken right beside the Balancing Rock.

Today there is a parking lot and a well-marked modern trail that leads 2.5 kilometres down to the Balancing Rock. The final descent is now via a set of stairs to a viewing platform from where you can get great photos of this picturesque natural phenomena.

Highway 217 goes right down the centre of Long Island, and other than the Balancing Rock trail there is only one other trail we are aware of that leads to the shoreline outside the villages at each end. This is a 0.8-kilometre trail that starts at Central Grove Provincial Park, which is close to the centre of Long Island. It leads to a viewing platform on the Bay of Fundy side that is well worth going to if the trail is not too muddy. Don't expect anything as spectacular as Balancing Rock.

At the far end of Long Island, around Northeast Cove, is the village of Freeport, which was founded by Loyalists in 1784. It's worth taking a walk around the cove on Water Street and Over Cove Road to get a sense of a working fishing village. The Islands Historical Society maintains the Islands Museum and Archives, which feature the history of Long and Brier Islands. There is

The Balancing Rock, a narrow vertical column of basalt, balanced precariously on its tip.

a special exhibit on Joshua Slocum of whom we will have more to say later.

The 1.3-kilometre Fundy View Trail starts behind the museum and starts up and then down to the Bay of Fundy shoreline with several viewpoints along the way. If you are interested in extending the hike, you can turn right and walk another couple of kilometres to Beautiful Cove. If the water is calm, and it often is here in summer, there is a good chance of spotting dolphins or whales from the shore.

On a more bizarre note, Freeport was the eventual destination of Brad Pitt's character in the zombie apocalypse movie *World War Z*. It was considered so remote and peaceful

Whale watching by zodiac.

that it was a perfect place to start rebuilding a world destroyed by zombies.

While there is plenty to see and do on Digby Neck and Long Island, our favourite place on this route is Brier Island, with its little village of Westport. The ferry ride across Grand Passage is always exciting, with views of the breeding bird colonies on Peter Island and the chance to see grey and harbour seals that frequent these waters. It genuinely feels as if you are going to the ends of the earth, and in a sense that is true. Brier Island is the most westerly point in the province.

If you love nature, then Brier Island is a place you must visit. It is the birding hotspot of Nova Scotia, the best place from which to see whales from shore or on an organized tour and the hiking trails will take you not only to some great scenery, but past some very rare and beautiful flowers. It has two lighthouses to visit and was the home of Joshua Slocum, who left Brier Island on the first ever solo navigation around the world from 1895–98, travelling over 74,000 kilometres in the process.

Where to start? We recommend spending at least two days on Brier Island to be able to get in whale watching and hiking at least some of the island's trails. Our choice of accommodations almost from the day it opened over 30 years ago has been the Brier Island Lodge, which has comfortable

Brier Island is a hot spot for birdlife, including the northern gannet (above), due to its position along the Atlantic Flyway migration route.

modern rooms and a good restaurant. You can't help but notice it sitting on a clifftop as you make the ferry crossing to Westport. The people who run it can help you arrange any of the things you might choose to do while visiting, starting with whale watching.

Brier Island was the first place we ever went whale watching and from that first time we were hooked. The mouth of the Bay of Fundy stretches roughly from Brier Island to Grand Manan Island on the New Brunswick side and marks the area where cold water upwells from below as the tide surges in twice each day. This upwelling brings tremendous amounts of plankton and krill near the surface, which attracts huge schools of herring and other small fish. All of these, from the tiny plankton to pollock and mackerel make this region of the Bay of Fundy a veritable smorgasbord for whales, dolphins, seals and seabirds.

If you are fortunate enough to go out on a calm day with little or no fog, which is likeliest in late summer, you can expect to see a sight that you will never forget. The most compelling thing to see is undoubtedly a breeching humpback whale throwing itself almost completely out of the water. A close second is seeing a finback whale, the second largest creature on earth, come close to the boat. The rarest is seeing one of the northern right whales that come here to raise their calves. Another is seeing a pod of dolphins porpoising alongside your boat.

It's not just the whales and dolphins that people come to see on these cruises. The pelagic birds at the mouth of the Bay of Fundy are legendary for their numbers and variety. Expect to see puffins, gannets torpedoing themselves into the water, several species of shearwaters, phalaropes and petrels as well as rarer species like jaegers and skuas.

Brier Island Lighthouse, also called Western Light, is the most westerly point in Nova Scotia and marks the spot where the Bay of Fundy officially begins.

Brier rose, for which the island is named.

Also, on the viewing menu are occasional sightings of basking sharks, bluefin tuna, several species of sea turtle, gigantic sunfish and even the occasional sperm whale.

There is no question that a whale-watching expedition on the Bay of Fundy is one of the two or three most exciting things you can do in this province. One decision you will need to make is whether to go on a five-hour cruise on a regular boat with up to 50 people or a 2.5 hour tour on a zodiac with up to a dozen people. The first one has more amenities, the second one gets you to the whales faster.

Back on dry land there's plenty more exploring to do. The Brier Island Coastal Trail runs four kilometres from Western Light to Big Pond Cove over ground that's been protected by the Nature Conservancy of Canada. It's one of the best coastal walks in Nova Scotia and offers more birding opportunities, particularly during migration season when this is the first, or the last place, for migrating birds to arrive or leave.

There are many more hiking and walking paths on Brier Island that beg to be explored.

When a whale breaches, up to 90 per cent of its body is above the surface.

If you stay near the shore there is a good chance of finding agate, jasper and amethyst, or you can go watch the breeding seal population at Seal Cove. One thing we never fail to do is to walk to the Joshua Slocum monument at the end of Water Street. It overlooks the bird sanctuary and lighthouse on Peter Island. It's also a short distance down to the beach, where you can see the basalt hexagons, some of which hang over your head from cliffs above.

As the most westerly point in Nova Scotia and one facing the Bay of Fundy, Brier Island may also be the best place to watch a sunset in Nova Scotia.

If you can plan a getaway for one of the long weekends during the summer or early fall, we can think of no place better than heading to Digby Neck for a two-night stay. Between the time you spend on the waters of the Bay of Fundy and the many short hikes you can take, you will come away reinvigorated — and we guarantee you will become hooked on whale watching.

USEFUL WEBSITES:

digbytrails.ca
Jerome: lifeasahuman.com/2011/arts-culture/history/the-story-of-jerome/
brierisland.com
novascotiawhalewatching.ca

13

EXPERIENCE THE **HABITATION AT PORT-ROYAL**

Alison at Port-Royal.

What we call Nova Scotia is in fact Mi'kma'ki, home to the Mi'kmaq people for thousands of years before the arrival of European settlers. When Europeans arrived, leading to the creation of what we now know as Nova Scotia and Canada, they first successfully settled in Port-Royal, with the establishment of the Habitation by Samuel de Champlain in 1605. In this chapter and the next we will explain why spending a few days in the town of Annapolis Royal to explore it and the surrounding area is a must-do for anyone who wants to understand how this province, as we know it today, came into being. It all starts with a little history lesson.

Most of us were taught in school that, leaving aside the brief Viking forays, the story of European exploration of what is now Canada began with the voyage of Italian Giovanni Caboto (John Cabot), sailing under the auspices of British King Henry VII. In 1497 he landed somewhere on either the shores of Cape Breton, where you can find a monument to him at Cabots Landing Provincial Park near Cape North, or in Newfoundland. Both provinces vie for being the site of this alleged 'first' landing. We were told in school that nothing much happened until Jacques Cartier sailed up the St. Lawrence River in 1534 and later in 1541 to found the first colony in Canada, Charlesbourg Royal at Cap-Rouge, just outside modern-day Quebec City. The colony failed, and was only rediscovered in 2006 when Italian ceramics and charred timbers were dated to a period that coincided with Cartier's last voyage.

Over 60 years passed before Champlain arrived in Nova Scotia in 1604, then explored the coasts of New Brunswick and Maine before attempting to create a settlement on St. Croix Island on the river that is now the border between Canada and the United States. This colony also failed. In 1605 Champlain found a much better location inside the protected waters of what is now the Annapolis Basin, which he named Port-Royal. This colony did succeed and, although it moved from its original location to present-day Annapolis Royal, was the gateway for the first European immigration to Canada — the French colonists who became known as the Acadians.

This is the type of history that is easy to grasp and tells a nice, linear, chronological story, but it's not accurate. Basque and Portuguese fishers had been coming to the shores of eastern Canada for centuries before Champlain and perhaps even before Columbus. They were exploiting the vast fisheries of the Grand Banks and those off Nova Scotia, and were using places like Canso to dry and salt their catches before returning to Europe in the autumn. At Red Bay, Labrador, they established a whaling station long before Cartier ever arrived. These were private commercial enterprises and those carrying them out had no desire to establish permanent colonies or even to broadcast the existence of these resources to others, particularly the monarchs who would likely seize them for their own profits.

While these early European landings in North America largely flew under the historical radar, they were very important

Statue of Samuel de Champlain.

in establishing relationships with local Indigenous peoples. By the time Champlain arrived in the Annapolis Basin to establish a permanent colony, the Mi'kmaq of the area were quite familiar with Europeans and willing to trade with them on the basis of mutual equality. The Mi'kmaq had knowledge to share and furs to trade in exchange for European goods that ultimately transformed their way of life. In other words, both sides had an interest in seeing that Port-Royal succeeded, which goes a long way to

The Habitation at Port-Royal. It was the first major reconstruction of a historic building undertaken by the Canadian government.

explaining why it succeeded where so many other early colonial settlements failed.

With these facts in mind, it's time to visit what is commonly referred to as the Habitation at Port-Royal. This is the best starting point for visiting the Annapolis Royal area. It is located a few miles off the Evangeline Trail (Highway 1) on the north shore of the Annapolis Basin, about a two-hour drive from Halifax. The turnoff is well signed and Granville Road passes through the pretty village of Granville Ferry on the way to the Port-Royal National Historic Site, as the Habitation is properly named. On the way is the very interesting North Hills Museum, housed in a 1760s farmhouse, which has an amazing collection of antiques acquired by the late Robert Patterson and bequeathed to the province upon his death. We recommend stopping here while you are in the area.

Port-Royal is not the only national historic site along this road. Before reaching the Habitation you will pass the Melanson Settlement National Historic Site, which marks the location of one of the earliest Acadian settlements in Nova Scotia. While almost all traces of the community are long gone, it is worth stopping to walk the short interpretive trail for the great view of the Annapolis Basin dykelands and to read the panels that explain the history of this place. We recommend stopping here after visiting the Habitation.

So what exactly is the Habitation and why is it important? What you see today is the first major reconstruction of a historic building undertaken by the Canadian government. The original Habitation was a complex of wooden buildings linked together in a rectangle surrounding an open area with a well in the middle. Originally built under the direction of Samuel de Champlain, it was intended to be a combination of a trading post for the collection of furs and the centre point for a colony that was to be set up along the banks of the Annapolis River. In 1603,

The central courtyard of the Habitation, with a well in the centre.

one Pierre Dugua de Mons (Sieur de Mons in our elementary history texts) was granted a monopoly on the fur trade over a huge swath of land in eastern North America by the French king, provided that he also established a colony there. Champlain was the de facto brains behind the scheme and designed and built the Habitation in 1605 on a site he picked out after the St. Croix Island settlement failed. Despite early travails that threatened to derail the project, including the temporary revocation of de Mons's monopoly in 1607, the Habitation was the catalyst for what would become the colony of Acadia.

In addition to its importance as the oldest successful European settlement in Canada, the Habitation has a number of other notable events associated with its brief tenure. Long before Champlain arrived the Mi'kmaq had a working relationship with European fishers, and that continued at Port-Royal. The Mi'kmaq chief in the area was the legendary Membertou, who became the first Indigenous person in Canada's history to convert to Catholicism and he did that right on this spot. That relationship between the Mi'kmaq people and the Catholic Church proved instrumental in the struggle for supremacy between the English and the French over what we now call Nova Scotia that began almost from the time the Habitation was completed. Membertou was left in charge of the buildings during the time that de Mons's charter was revoked, and the putative colonists were returned to France. He kept it in good order until de Mons's successor, Sieur de Poutrincourt returned in 1610 with a new group of settlers.

Speaking of good order, the Habitation is also known as the place where the oldest social club in North America, the Order of Good Cheer, was founded. Intended to break up the boredom of the long winter days and as an antidote to 'land sickness' (which was actually scurvy, a disease caused by a lack of vitamin C), Champlain decreed

The Coat of Arms of Sieur de Mons, Sieur de Poutrincourt, and Henri IV, King of France when the Habitation was built in 1605.

that each member take a turn in preparing food, drink and entertainment for their fellow inhabitants. Among the consequences was the writing and production of the first play in Canada, *The Theatre of Neptune*, by Marc Lescarbot. The Order of Good Cheer still exists, although now called the more banal Order of the Good Time, and you can become an honorary member at a number of Nova Scotia tourism offices as long as you spend three days in the province. We are both proud members.

You can also pick up an Order of Good Cheer Trail passport at Port-Royal, which as of 2019 has 72 locations where you can sample Nova Scotia wines, beers, ciders and distilled spirits.

In 1613, Samuel Argall sailed north from the British settlement of Jamestown, Virginia, intent on wreaking as much havoc as possible on the new French colonies. He entered the Annapolis Basin and found the Habitation empty, all the inhabitants being upriver doing who knows what. That made it very easy for him to burn it to the ground, and it stayed that way for the next 327 years. Harriet Taber Richardson was an American from Cambridge, Massachusetts,

In the wigwam just outside the Habitation walls, interpreters offer the songs and legends of the Mi'kmaq.

who spent her summers in the Annapolis Royal area and had a fascination with Champlain. When she learned that her countrymen were the ones who had destroyed the Habitation, she determined to correct this historical wrong and began a fundraising campaign to rebuild it. While it was not initially successful because of the onset of the Great Depression, in 1939 the Government of Canada bought into

it and used the money raised plus its own funds to rebuild the Habitation along the lines of Champlain's original drawings and descriptions. It is recognized as one of the most significant historical reconstructions undertaken anywhere. It now seems as much a part of the natural landscape as if it had been here from 1605 onward.

After paying the Parks Canada entry fee, take the time to circle the outside of

The Common Room and dining hall. Here, Samuel de Champlain began a social club called "L'Ordre de Bon Temps" (the Order of Good Cheer).

the building to get an appreciation of its size and complexity, considering what little materials the original builders would have had available to them. If possible, you should plan your visit to coincide with the appearance of Samuel de Champlain every Tuesday afternoon in the summer months. There will also be a Mi'kmaq interpreter on site during this time.

There are a number of interpretive and historical markers around the grounds. Step inside a wigwam, where you can watch a Mi'kmaq artist creating original porcupine quillwork items. It is almost a lost art that requires hours and hours to finish even the smallest of items.

You enter the Habitation through a small open gate over which three coats of arms are posted. On top is that of the Kingdom of France and Navarre and below are those of Sieur de Mons and Sieur de Poutrincourt.

Once inside, tour the rooms in any order you wish. These include the tiny chapel, the forge, the apothecary's, private quarters for gentlemen and much more cramped spaces on the second floor for the hoi polloi, as well as the fur-trading room, which has pelts from many of the species brought to the Habitation by Mi'kmaq hunters.

One room that shouldn't be missed is the dining hall, which was where the events central to the Order of Good Cheer took place.

This is where Samuel de Champlain will make his appearance and for almost an hour relate not only the history of this place, but much more about the early exploration of North America, relations with the Indigenous people, rivalries amongst the French, and other topics, much of which provided the background for this chapter.

Back outside, walk down to Parks Canada's red chairs to gaze out over the

The storeroom full of pelts such as beaver, muskrat, otter, fox, wolf and raccoon. These the Mi'kmaq traded in return for axes and knives, copper or iron kettles, cloth, beads and iron fish hooks.

Annapolis Basin with the famous Habitation and Samuel de Champlain at your back.

If you think that the Habitation was not a success because it only lasted eight years before being torched, think again. The French knew they were onto something good here and returned, but to a slightly different location in what is now Annapolis Royal on the other side of the river. Read Chapter 14 to finish the story of Annapolis Royal.

WHAT YOU NEED TO KNOW:

Name: Port-Royal
Address: 53 Historic Lane, Granville Ferry, NS B0S 1K0
Websites: pc.gc.ca/en/lhn-nhs/ns/portroyal
pc.gc.ca/en/lhn-nhs/ns/melanson
northhills.novascotia.ca/
novascotia.com/eat-drink/good-cheer-trail
Season: May to October
Opening times: 9–5:30 pm
Price: <$5
Other note: Enjoy a guided tour
Classic photo op (Instagram worthy!): Champlain's Order of the Good Cheer dining hall

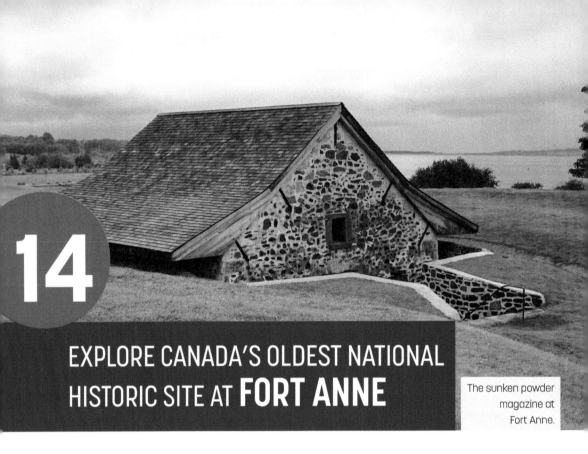

14

EXPLORE CANADA'S OLDEST NATIONAL HISTORIC SITE AT **FORT ANNE**

The sunken powder magazine at Fort Anne.

Fort Anne is considered by many historians to be the finest surviving example of a colonial fort in North America. When the government of Canada instituted its National Historic Sites program in 1917, it was a no-brainer to make Fort Anne the first such site. That program has grown to over 970 sites in every province and territory, but Nova Scotians can be proud that it was one of their historic places that led the way. Every Nova Scotian and visitor to our province needs to visit this hallowed ground. We have visited here many times over the years and find something new and interesting on every visit.

Fort Anne is intrinsically linked with the town of Annapolis Royal. You can walk right onto the main street from the fort. Driving along the Evangeline Trail through the town, you will notice the large, whitewashed, wooden Officers' Quarters, which was constructed in 1797 and is now the fort's museum. For over a hundred years, it has been welcoming visitors and has evolved from a place with a few muskets and uniforms on display to a full-fledged modern multi-media experience that tells in words, pictures and artifacts the story of Fort Anne.

The fort is administered by Parks Canada, which has also evolved in its methods of presenting a national historic site. A variety of programs are offered that appeal to people of all ages, including several types of guided tours — or you can rent a tablet for $5, which will greatly enhance a self-guided tour. We

The 1797 officers' quarters in the centre of the fort house the museum.

highly recommend taking the white glove tour, where a maximum of ten people are taken on a behind-the-scenes tour of many of the fort's most precious artifacts that are not on display to the general public. Combine this with a general tour of the museum and then a walk around the grounds and you'll have more than enough to occupy you for a morning or afternoon. After that, there is time to explore more of Annapolis Royal, including its famous historic gardens.

Before heading to Fort Anne, which is about a two-hour drive from Halifax, learning a little about the history of the area will make for a more enjoyable visit.

The fort is built on a natural defensive position where the Annapolis River and Allain's Creek drain into the Annapolis Basin, creating a triangle of land surrounded by water on two sides. The only way into the

Annapolis Basin from the sea is the narrow Digby Gut that cuts a channel through North Mountain, about 20 kilometres from this site. By positioning sentries at the opening, the occupants of the fort would have had plenty of time to prepare for any attack coming their way. It wasn't just the English and French who knew this, but the Mi'kmaq people as well. There is evidence that they occupied the area as many as 3,000 years ago.

The historical, as opposed to the archaeological, era at Fort Anne began with establishment of Port-Royal in 1605, which we have included in Chapter 13. It was located directly on the shore of the Annapolis Basin in a not particularly defensible spot, which the French found out when English colonists from Jamestown, Virginia, burned it to the ground in 1613, setting off a century and a half of bloody conflict.

One of the 19 cannons spread out over the grounds.

There followed a brief, but for Nova Scotia, very important interregnum. King James I of England granted Sir William Alexander all of the land that currently comprises the three Maritime Provinces and the Gaspé Peninsula of Quebec. It was to be named New Scotland, but the charter was in Latin, so the name became Nova Scotia. You can view a copy of this document in the fort's museum. Alexander's son landed a group of would-be Scots settlers here in 1629, but the experiment fizzled, and the land was ceded to France in 1632. Despite that failure, they did come up with the coat-of-arms and the flag, which we use today.

The French returned in 1636, took over and expanded the fort the Scots had started and renamed the place Port-Royal. The first Acadian settlers arrived here and over the next century spread out through many parts of Nova Scotia, New Brunswick and Prince Edward Island, creating the French colony of Acadia. This did not go unnoticed in English circles, and in 1654 and 1690 Port-Royal was attacked and captured by British forces from New England. Each time it was returned to France, which decided enough was enough and commissioned a French engineer to create a modern star-shaped fort in the style developed by Sebastién de

Dale exiting the underground powder magazine in a corner of the fortifications.

Vauban for King Louis XIV. Most of what you see today at Fort Anne dates from this period. Inside the museum you can view an interactive map that shows the many changes made to the fortifications over the years.

A good fort is only as good as the people defending it, as the French found out in 1710 when a force of 35 ships and 2,000 men entered the Annapolis Basin and began besieging Port-Royal. Greatly outnumbered, the French surrendered and this time lost Acadia for good, as confirmed by the Treaty of Utrecht in 1713.

That didn't stop the fighting at what was now called Annapolis Royal, which was attacked numerous times between 1722 and 1755, all without success. That latter year saw the deportation of over 1,600 Acadians from the landing below the fort and the subsequent

arrival of the New England Planters, who settled on the lands involuntarily vacated by their former owners. Dale's mother's family, the Allens were among those who arrived at the spot you can see today from the walls of the fort. In 1783, over 3,000 Loyalists fleeing the newly independent United States of America first landed at this spot.

After the end of the Seven Years' War, the French lost control of their possessions in Canada and peace at long last seemed to come to the area — but not for long. There was one last attack in 1781, when American privateers successfully took over the fort and the town for a short period. The threat from the Americans prompted the British to build the Officers' Barracks in 1797, but the newly renamed Fort Anne was never threatened again and gradually the place fell into a long

Detail of the Fort Anne Heritage Tapestry.

reconstruction of an Acadian home, the copy of the 1621 charter, the key to the fort and a portrait of King Louis XIV that gradually turns into Queen Anne as you walk past it.

One must-see attraction in the museum is the Fort Anne Heritage Tapestry, which, in our opinion, is one of the most remarkable and intricate artifacts in the entire province. It is an 8.5 by 5.5 metre tapestry that contains over three million stitches made by over 100 volunteers, including Queen Elizabeth. It has an astonishing beauty that traces the history of the area in four sections, from Port-Royal to the present day.

Take the short, guided tapestry tour that will point out various aspects of the stitchwork including the portion that Queen Elizabeth worked on.

The white glove tour takes visitors into parts of the museum that are not open to the general public. Highlights of this tour include a kilt worn by a Nova Scotian at Vimy Ridge which still has mud from the trenches on it.

There is just as much to explore on the Fort Anne grounds and again, we recommend taking the guided tour to get a better appreciation of the history that took place here and the nature of a Vauban fortification. There are 19 cannons spread out over the grounds, and it is interesting to look at each one to determine if they were of English or French origin by examining the royal markings.

There are several places to sit in the Parks Canada's red chairs and enjoy the view of the Annapolis Basin, or you can stroll the 750-metre perimeter walk and see the bust of Sieur de Mons, the founder of Port-Royal. The pamphlet *100 Things to Do at Fort Anne* lists over 20 things to look for while exploring the grounds.

torpor. Most of the buildings inside the fort, including the blockhouse, were demolished, and in 1854 the British left for good. Fort Anne languished for another 70 years until its historical importance was recognized and it became a national historic site in 1917 — and has been treated with the reverence it deserves ever since.

The presentations and layout of the museum have changed considerably over time. Today the museum tells the story of Fort Anne in a chronological sequence that follows a path from room to room, starting with the Mi'kmaq. Highlights include the

The Sally Port. This entrance into the fort grounds was used by British soldiers.

For some people the most interesting thing on the grounds will be the cemetery, which is the oldest in Canada — the oldest grave dates to 1720. There were over 2,000 people buried here, but there are only 234 tombstones. That is more than enough to keep most visitors occupied in trying to decipher the faded inscriptions and fancy stone carvings.

Visiting the cemetery also provides a perfect excuse for spending the night in Annapolis Royal, which has some of the finest old inns in Nova Scotia. Every night at 9:30 p.m. from June 1 to October 15, candlelit graveyard tours are hosted by heritage interpreter Alan Melanson, who doubles as Samuel de Champlain at the Habitation at Port-Royal during the day. The tours last an hour and fifteen minutes, cost only $10 and don't require reservations. It's the perfect way to end a tour of probably the most historic piece of property in Nova Scotia, if not all of Canada.

WHAT YOU NEED TO KNOW:

Name: Fort Anne
Address: 323 St George Street, Annapolis Royal, NS B0S 1A0
Websites: pc.gc.ca/en/lhn-nhs/ns/fortanne
tourannapolisroyal.com/graveyard.html
Season: May to October
Opening times: All day
Price: <$5
Other note: Take the White Glove Tour
Classic photo op (Instagram worthy!): A view of the ramparts

15

MARVEL AT THE LANDSCAPE
OF **GRAND PRÉ**

Grand Pré National Historic Site.

The small village of Grand Pré is a five-minute drive east of Wolfville and about an hour from Halifax on Highway 101. Most people are aware that Grand Pré was the principal site of the deportation of the Acadians or the "Grand Dérangement" as the people displaced refer to it. However, there are a lot of other reasons to visit Grand Pré. These include touring the 11 sites identified as important to understanding how the landscape came into being, the many wineries or cideries in the area, birding the fields and beaches and learning how Henry Wadsworth Longfellow's fictional poem "Evangeline" helped ensure the land was not lost to development before anyone appreciated what a gem Grand Pré is.

In 2012, the Landscape of Grand Pré was designated as a UNESCO World Heritage site — the 16th in Canada and third in Nova Scotia. Obtaining such a designation requires a site to meet a series of extremely difficult and, in many cases, unique criteria, and only occurs after years of study and on-site visits by experts in history, geography, anthropology and other disciplines. As of 2020, there are only 1,121 of these sites, spread over 167 countries, so having three in a place as small as Nova Scotia is quite an achievement; Ontario only has one. The UNESCO website describes why the Landscape of Grand Pré received its designation:

The Landscape of Grand Pré is an exceptional living agricultural landscape, claimed from the sea in the 17th century and still in use today applying the same technology and the same community-based management. Grand Pré is also the iconic place of remembrance of the Acadians who lived in harmony with the native Mi'Kmaq people before the Expulsion which began in 1755. Its memorial constructions form the centre of the symbolic re-appropriation of the land of their origins by the Acadians, in the 20th century, in a spirit of peace and cultural sharing with the local area community.

The starting point for any visit to Grand Pré is usually at the excellent Visitor Centre. You'll likely be greeted at the door by an Acadian fiddler dressed in traditional clothing and wearing the wooden sabots that were the footwear of choice for the common folk. There is an entry fee of just under $8, but we recommend paying another $4 to join one of the daily guided tours that leaves each morning in English and in French (check the website for the latest information on times). These tours last about 45 minutes and you'll learn a lot more about Grand Pré than you will by walking around on your own.

The Visitor Centre has a multi-media presentation, which provides good background before you walk through the large exhibit room dominated by a recreation of the dyke and aboiteau system and a model of the Acadian settlement at Grand Pré. An aboiteau, not to be confused with an abattoir, is a type of sluice that let water drain out at low tide and prevented it from coming back in at high tide, thus over time completely draining the marsh and creating an entirely new landscape.

Leaving the Visitor Centre through the back door, you will see the five figure *Deportation Sculpture*, depicting an Acadian

Acadian fiddler, wearing traditional wooden sabots.

family on the run from the British. It is quite moving and very photogenic.

A pathway then leads to a crossing of the Harvest Moon Trailway, which is on the railbed of the old Dominion Atlantic Railway and can be followed on foot or by bike all the way to Annapolis Royal, 110 kilometres away. Near the crossing point there once stood a railway station that brought visitors to Grand Pré and was the main reason Grand Pré became such a famous tourist site in the first place. In 1917 John Frederic Herbin, a successful jeweler from nearby Wolfville (his great grandson still runs the store), sold the parcel of land

The memorial church, built in the traditional Quebec manner.

that is now most of the Grand Pré National Historic Site to the Dominion Atlantic Railway. An old well of undetermined origin was on the land and a group of ancient willows that Herbin believed were first planted by his Acadian ancestors. He made one stipulation — that the railway must maintain the area in its original condition as a park. Shortly after the sale, railway owners decided to build a monument on site to the Acadians. In 1922 the iconic stone building in the form of a church was opened to the public. Most people mistakenly believe it is a church, but it was never consecrated and was always intended to be a monument.

At roughly the same time, the most famous statue in Nova Scotia — that of Longfellow's fictional Evangeline — was erected in front of the church. "Evangeline" was the most popular of his extensive works and was almost single-handedly responsible for a worldwide interest in Acadia and the Acadians. Much as *Anne of Green Gables* put Prince Edward Island on the literary tourism map, so did "Evangeline" for Nova Scotia. The railway added a Victorian garden, duck pond and walkways around the bucolic utopia that Longfellow described in his poem and it was a hit. Thousands of people came by railway to visit Grand Pré and detrained at this very spot.

No matter how many times we visit Grand Pré we never get tired of this scene. There is something about the brilliant statue and the symmetry of the stone monument with its almost impossibly steep spire that is, well to excuse the bad pun, inspiring. Inside there is a group of six paintings illustrating the six stages of the expulsion, as well as a diorama showing the embarkation that took place in 1755 not more than a few kilometres from this spot.

The British did such a good job of destroying the Grand Pré settlement after the expulsion that even with today's most sophisticated archaeological tools, no one has been able to find remnants of the church that records show was nearby. An old burial ground has been located, but excavation of old graves is a complicated and controversial matter, so little work has been undertaken there. It's as if the original settlers of Grand Pré were wiped off the map.

After touring inside, several things you should see include the reconstructed forge with its great view of the reclaimed lands, the bust of Longfellow, the Herbin cross and the old well. Returning to the Visitor Centre, make sure to check out the gift shop for all things Acadian. Then it's time to explore the other points of interest in

Statue representing Longfellow's fictional Evangeline.

the Landscape of Grand Pré, starting with the site of the massacre of over 70 British troops in 1747 by a combined French and Indigenous force that attacked in the middle of a blinding snowstorm. Although the local inhabitants were not involved, it created an air of suspicion between the British and the Acadians that may have contributed to the decision to expel them eight years later. This monument is just after the turnoff from Highway 1 to Grand Pré.

For the most part there is good signage indicating where to turn down side roads to

Panels inside the memorial church depicting the expulsion of the Acadians.

find the most important sites. One of these leads to Horton Landing at the mouth of the Gaspereau River. This was both the actual site of the deportation of the Grand Pré inhabitants and the landing point of the first New England Planters five years later. Both events are marked by historical markers and a cross.

Don't miss a visit to Evangeline Beach, which you'll reach after driving straight through the heart of the reclaimed land. On the way you'll pass the tiny North Grand Pré Community Church, which is worth a quick stop. At the end of the road is Evangeline Beach, one of the most important birding spots in Nova Scotia. From mid-July through August up to a million shorebirds make their way here to fatten up on mud shrimp on their only stop on a 4,000-kilometre migration from the Arctic to points south. If you arrive here at high tide when the birds are compressed into a small area between the shore and the small cliffs, you will see thousands of birds take flight and put on an aerial display that is phenomenal to see. Watch the birds from a safe distance so as not to disturb them unnecessarily. There are numerous interpretive panels explaining why Evangeline Beach has been designated an Important Bird and Biodiversity Area.

If you get here at low tide, all is not lost. The tide rises and falls an incredible 16–17 metres. When it's out, it seems like you can

Evangeline Beach - a birder's paradise and a great spot to watch the sun go down.

walk forever to reach the water, however you will get very muddy (for a lot of people that's the point). If you don't want to get muddy or are not a birder, enjoy another of the iconic views in the Landscape of Grand Pré — Cape Blomidon, which lies just across the Minas Basin.

By now it is time to sample some of the bounty of the Landscape of Grand Pré, and there's no better place to do this than at nearby Domaine de Grand Pré — the oldest farm winery in Atlantic Canada. The Stutz family came to Canada from Switzerland and recognized the potential of the Annapolis Valley, and particularly the Grand Pré area, for growing grapes.

They were not the first to realize this. The first grapes grown north of the Spanish Empire (which is pretty well all of the United States and Canada) were grown by the Acadians. They had a thriving viniculture in Grand Pré before the British arrived. The British preferred cider and let the vineyards grow wild and eventually disappear, replacing many of them with apple orchards. Now both wine and cider are produced in quantities unimaginable only a few decades ago. Better yet, the quality has steadily risen to the point that Nova Scotia wineries and cideries are winning awards around the world.

Domaine de Grand Pré has a beautiful location overlooking the Grand Pré area and

Aerial view of the Domaine de Grand Pré.

they have enhanced it with wonderful gardens and one of the top 20 vineyard restaurants in the world, housed in an architecturally stunning stone and wood building. At Le Caveau you can sample the cornucopia of products that are raised or caught in this area. The outdoor section of the restaurant, the Pergola, is the perfect place for lunch while visiting the area. Two favourites are the lobster, scallop and shrimp chowder and the halibut and shrimp cakes. On a hot summer day there's no better way to wash these down than with one of the local wines or a glass of ice-cold Annapolis cider from nearby Wolfville.

Parks Canada red chairs, with views across the Grand Pré landscape and the Minas Basin.

The last stop on this whirlwind tour of the Landscape of Grand Pré can be reached by motor vehicle, but we prefer to walk to it through the vineyard at Domaine de Grand Pré. It's not far and the walking is easy. Here you will find the aptly named View Park, where the UNESCO world heritage site was dedicated.

WHAT YOU NEED TO KNOW:

Name: Grand Pré National Historic Site
Address: 2205 Grand Pré Rd, Grand Pré, NS BOP 1MO
Websites: landscapeofgrandpre.ca/home.html
pc.gc.ca/en/lhn-nhs/ns/grandpre
novascotia.com/see-do/trails/harvest-moon-trailway/7648
grandprewines.com
Season: May to October
Price: <$10
Other note: Enhanced programs July and August
Classic photo op (Instagram worthy!): Evangeline in front of the Memorial Church

16

EXPERIENCE THE **WORLD'S HIGHEST TIDES**

Smashing into the tidal bore.

No book on Nova Scotia would be complete without mention of the world's highest tides that occur in the Bay of Fundy, which the province shares with New Brunswick. Twice a day the bay receives an injection of sea water equal to the flow of all the rivers on Earth as the water rises as much as 50 feet from low to high tide. That's the equivalent of a five-storey building. The tides are so high because the bay is shaped like a funnel with two openings, Chignecto Bay and the Minas Basin, that get narrower and narrower near their ends. The huge amount of water is forced into an ever-decreasing space, which means that it has only one place to go — up.

The world record for the highest tides occurs at a picturesque place called Burntcoat

Head in Hants County. Visit at low tide to get an idea of just how far out the water recedes. Ideally, one can walk out hundreds of metres from the high-tide line just as the tide begins to turn and starts coming in. It goes at a walking pace, and you can walk back to the shore with the incoming tide as a companion — just don't make the mistake of standing on a sandstone boulder and watching the waters rise around you. In a matter of minutes, you might find yourself having to swim for your life.

Burntcoat Head features a modern recreation of the lighthouse that once stood here. You can climb to the top for a view of Flowerpot Island, once home to the first lighthouse in this area. For

more information and low tide times visit burntcoatheadpark.ca.

You'll find lots of information on the Fundy tides as well as the history of this area, including the tragic story of Noel and Marie Doiron. They were Acadian settlers who built many of the dykes in this area, as well as raising eight children. They were expelled by the British during the Grand Dérangement and put aboard a ship to England, which foundered in the English Channel within sight of land. Noel, Marie and all of their children were drowned.

Another natural phenomenon associated with the Bay of Fundy tides is a tidal bore — a wave created by the force of the incoming tide as it pushes its way upstream on one of the many rivers that flow into the Minas

Twice each day the Bay of Fundy fills and empties its 160 billion tons of water. Burntcoat Head has an average tide of 47.5 feet (14.5 m). The ocean floor exposed at Flowerpot Island (top).

The lookoff from the historic South Maitland Bridge, built over the Shubenacadie River by the Midland Railway in 1901.

Basin and Chignecto Bay. Now just because the tide will rise 50 feet, don't think that a tidal bore is like a tsunami. It takes six hours to rise up that high. During the highest tides, it can be as high as six to nine feet and move fast enough that it can be surfed. In 2013 two Californian surfers rode the tidal bore on the Petticodiac River in New Brunswick for an incredible 29 kilometres, from the mouth of the river right into the city of Moncton.

In perfect honesty, a tidal bore can be just that, a bore. Inevitably it is much smaller than people expect and goes by so quickly that it leaves one wondering what all the fuss was about. One major exception to our hesitation in recommending tidal-bore watching is the Fundy Tidal Interpretive Centre just south of Maitland on the Shubenacadie River.

The tidal bore on the Shubenacadie can, at times of very high tides, be quite large. The remnants of the old railway bridge that once spanned the river at this spot is the perfect place to view it. Here you will also find interpreters to answer your questions

other obstructions in the river. Participants need to wear helmets and are expected to paddle to assist the helmsman/guide. If you fall out of a whitewater raft or it tips over, you will be swept downriver and, depending on the severity of the rapids, you could be in serious peril.

With tidal bore rafting the rapids are not caused by underlying rocks, but rather by the force of the salt water being pushed upriver with the incoming tide colliding with the freshwater flowing seaward. The rapids are ephemeral — they are whipped up and last for only about 15 or 20 minutes at each site. You do not need to wear a helmet while tidal bore rafting and you don't need to paddle. The raft is propelled upriver by an outboard motor, and if you fall overboard it's no big deal as you are not going to hit a rock or get jammed under a submerged log. In fact, some people like to shoot the rapids without a raft.

There are currently five companies providing tidal bore rafting on the Shubenacadie River and they all provide an excellent experience, as each takes you to the same sets of rapids. The operators co-operate with each other and make sure that every group gets a number of runs through each set of rapids. The trip we describe here was with River Runners (riverrunnersns.com), which operates out of the historic village of Maitland almost right across from the W.D. Lawrence House, now a provincial museum (lawrencehouse.novascotia.ca/). Maitland was once one of the biggest ship-building communities in North America and it was here that the largest wooden sailing ship ever built in Canada was launched. If you have an afternoon departure, we highly recommend arriving early and visiting this

about the Bay of Fundy tides and why they are so dramatic. The bridge lookoff is the perfect place to watch tidal bore rafters go by. If you don't want to join them, then you can wave to them from this elevated spot as they surge by below. For more information on viewing the Shubenacadie tidal bore go to easthants.ca/explore/attractions-events/tidal-bore-rafting.

For us, the best way to experience the Bay of Fundy tides is to go on a tidal bore rafting trip on the Shubenacadie River. Tidal bore rafting is completely different than whitewater rafting, which involves going downriver over rapids created by rocks and

Zodiacs ready for a tidal bore rafting trip.

museum to learn more about Nova Scotia's ship-building heritage.

River Runners is the tidal bore rafting company closest to the mouth of the river, and your journey with them starts on the Bay of Fundy.

The first thing to decide in booking a tidal bore rafting trip is how much excitement you can handle. The start of the incoming tidal bore can be predicted with great accuracy and it begins about 40 minutes later each day. The intensity varies with the phases of the moon, with the highest tides during new and full moons and the lowest at half-moon. Basically, there are three types of tidal bore experiences depending on the strength of the incoming tide. The mildest tides provide a much more modest tidal bore and gentler, smaller rapids than the average tides and the extreme tides. The latter create truly wild rapids as high as 10 or 12 feet, and you will

never forget the ride. The extreme tide rides are not for the faint of heart, the very young or anyone who hasn't the strength to hold onto the raft's side ropes. You will find a link on the River Runners website that indicates the degree of severity of the tides on any given day.

The other decision to make is whether to take the two-hour or the three-hour excursion. The two-hour excursion goes as far as the highway bridge crossing the Shubenacadie at South Maitland, and will provide enough excitement for most people. The three-hour trip continues upriver to two of the largest rapids on the river. Once these subside it's a 30 minute ride back to the base.

Tidal bore rafters are fitted with personal flotation devices that are checked for proper fit by the guides before setting out. Yellow rain jackets are offered, but not mandatory. You do need to wear clothes that are okay to get

Surfing the tidal bore on the Shubenacadie River. Those seated at the front of the boat get the wettest!

soaked and stained rust red from the river's muddy water. Take only waterproof cameras, as every piece of equipment you take aboard the raft will be thoroughly soaked. You can lock your valuables in your car and leave the keys at the reception desk.

Each raft holds up to eight people plus the guide. Courtesy dictates that the passengers frequently change position so that everyone who wants to gets a chance to be up front where the action is the wildest and wettest.

Since you are starting out at low tide the rafts will be about 40 feet down from the shoreline, where you will return in a few hours.

Once everyone is aboard the rafts, head out onto the Bay of Fundy to await the arrival of the tidal bore. It's usually very calm and peaceful out here and you may be wondering when the excitement is going to begin. After about 15 minutes the bore can be spotted on

the horizon as it approaches at a pretty good clip. Then the adventure starts as the rafts surf the bore as it moves upriver.

There will be a few passes as the rafts slam into the bore.

After a number of runs through the tidal bore, the guides let it go on its way where it will be met by other rafting groups. Now it is time to attack the first set of rapids that materialize before your eyes in the wake of the passing tidal bore. These first rapids are pretty tame, and you still might be thinking that tidal bore rafting is not as exciting as whitewater rafting.

That impression might last a while, as the next part of the trip involves pulling up onto a very large island near the mouth of the river and getting out to stretch your feet. But then you notice that the island is rapidly disappearing as the rising tide is covering the sand at an incredibly fast rate. It's a very

This area is home to one of the largest concentrations of bald eagles on the planet.

strange feeling to be standing on what seems to be solid ground only to see it disappear beneath your feet in seconds. By the time you get back in the rafts, the water is above your knees and rising fast.

Now comes the real excitement, as the guide steers the raft through rapids that make the first set look like waves in a bathtub. Everybody gets completely soaked and screams are *de rigeur* each time the raft plunges into increasingly larger waves.

At times the raft will be almost completely full of water and you might wonder how it stays afloat, but the guides perform expert manoeuvres that quickly drain the water before the next pass. On the three-hour trip there are about seven or eight sets of rapids and the guide usually makes three passes through each one, so you definitely get your money's worth of watery thrills. In addition to the rapids, you might come across a genuine whirlpool large enough to spin the raft around.

About halfway through the outing, the guides will stop at a relatively calm spot to let anyone who wants to jump overboard and

Mud sliding on the red clay banks of the Shubenacadie River. (Image courtessty of Shubenacadie River Adventure Tours.)

float upriver for a spell or even give you the chance to slide down mud banks. The water is surprisingly warm, and it's perfectly safe.

Even without the excitement of surfing the tidal bore, watching the island disappear and attacking the rapids, this would be a great trip. The mouth of the Shubenacadie is an incredibly scenic area with high sandstone cliffs in places and further upriver a fault line that once separated tectonic plates. In places, the stains in the sandstone created by the presence of copper give a distinctly green appearance to the otherwise rust-red cliffs. Add to this the fact that the area is home to one of the largest concentrations of bald eagles on Earth (you're guaranteed to see some nests) and you have a naturalist's dream.

On returning to headquarters, there are hot showers, hot chocolate and freshly baked cookies awaiting — a fitting end to a unique and thrilling adventure.

WHAT YOU NEED TO KNOW:

Name: Shubenacadie River Runners
Address: 8681 Highway 215, Maitland NS BON 1TO
Websites: burntcoatheadpark.ca easthants.ca/explore/fundy-tidal-interpretive-centre/ riverrunnersns.com raftingcanada.ca lawrencehouse.novascotia.ca
Season: May to September
Depends on the tides (call ahead)
Price: $65.00 for two-hour tour, $85.00 for three-hour tour
Other note: Wear your old clothes and tight-fitting shoes!
Classic photo op (Instagram worthy!): View from the disused railway bridge over the Shubenacadie River

Anderson's Cove.

17

HIKE AND KAYAK THE
THREE SISTERS

The legendary high tides of the Bay of Fundy are known for creating unique natural phenomena, including tidal bores, whirlpools that appear and disappear in minutes and harbours where boats tied up to wharves in 20 feet of water are high and dry on the ocean floor hours later. Hall's Harbour in King's County is probably the best place to see this last wonder of nature. Many people are familiar with Hopewell Rocks on the New Brunswick side of the bay, where you can walk on the ocean floor at low tide and kayak through the standing rock formations at high tide, but did you know you can do this in Nova Scotia as well? It takes a little more time and effort, but visiting the Three Sisters rock formation in Cape Chignecto

Provincial Park at high and low tide is one of the best outdoor experiences Nova Scotia has to offer.

Cape Chignecto Provincial Park, the largest in Nova Scotia, preserves one of the most spectacular stretches of wilderness shoreline in the world and yet is one of the least visited places in the province (and one of the most remote). The most dramatic feature of the Cape Chignecto area is a rock formation known as the Three Sisters. According to Mi'kmaq traditional lore there were three female sorceresses who were capable of shapeshifting into various animals at will. To play a trick on Kluscap, also known as Glooscap, the sisters turned themselves into wolves and chased away a moose that he

Boats at West Apple River.

Kayaks on the beach at Eatonville.

was hunting. Kluscap did not think this was funny and turned the three sorceresses into stone, where they remain to this day.

The park is home to a three-day circular hiking trail (in addition to shorter trails) that starts out on the ocean floor at beautiful Red Rocks, just outside Advocate Harbour, and rises to the top of cliffs that tower 600 feet above the bay below. It passes through one of the largest remaining old-growth forests in Nova Scotia and somewhat paradoxically drops down to coastal estuaries, where forgotten communities like Eatonville are mere remnants of a once-booming lumbering and ship-building business. But you don't need to hike for three days to get bucket-list worthy views. You can park at the Eatonville Visitor Centre (which is unfortunately permanently closed) and explore the area on foot via two trail systems — one that leads to

a view of the Three Sisters and the other to equally worthy Squally Point lookoff.

From Halifax it's a good three-hour drive to Cape Chignecto, so we recommend not trying to make this a day trip. Stay at least one night in the Advocate Harbour area, especially if you are going to do both the hiking and kayaking. The Driftwood Park Retreat has some great cottages right on Advocate Beach, where you will get views of Cape Chignecto from right outside the door.

These sea stacks known as the Three Sisters are remnants of a rocky headland that was eroded by the wind and waves.

The Wild Caraway restaurant in town is one of the best in the province and people drive from Halifax just to eat here, so it's a bonus to be able to have a couple of meals at this great little spot.

From Advocate Harbour, take the West Apple River Road to get to the trailheads. You'll be driving through one of the least visited areas of Nova Scotia and the road gets progressively worse the further you go, but there is some seriously good scenery along the way. You will also pass by Spicer's Cove, where the kayaking trips launch.

Follow the sign for the turnoff to the Eatonville Visitor Centre. There is a small parking lot here and both trailheads are well marked. If you do the kayaking tour you will be able to look up from the cove below and see the Visitor Centre on top of the cliff.

The trail to the Three Sisters lookoff is 2.6 kilometres return and is not particularly difficult, but hiking boots are a must if you are going to make the difficult descent down to the shore. Remember you can only do that at low tide, so read your tide tables in advance.

Long before you get to the Three Sisters, you will be blown away by views of Anderson's Cove.

The star attraction is the Three Sisters and they do not disappoint. Notice how at least two of the three stacks seem to have the shape of a woman's face. It is possible to scramble and bushwhack your way down to the shoreline and walk between the rock formations, but there is no defined trail and we cannot recommend it. People have had to be rescued by helicopter after becoming trapped by the fast-moving incoming tide.

Returning to the Visitor Centre, the trail in the opposite direction is 3.1 kilometres return and leads to a rare geological formation at Squally Point — a raised beach that is 40 metres above sea level.

We cannot stress enough how important it is to visit the Three Sisters by kayak as part of an organized tour, and not on your own. The tides of the Bay of Fundy are notoriously treacherous when they are incoming or outgoing and can create conditions that can become life threatening within minutes to someone in a kayak. Nova Shores Sea Kayaking in Advocate Harbour has been leading tours in the Cape Chignecto area for many years and have an impeccable safety record. Most people choose to do this in a tandem kayak, as Dale did with fellow adventurer Ryan Barry a few years ago.

The tour launches from Spicer's Cove and takes six hours, three of which involve paddling. While anyone in reasonably good shape can do this tour, depending on the waves and the tide, it can become very tiring, which is why a tandem kayak is the best option. There is a lunch stop at Eatonville Beach that gives a chance to explore what little is left of what was once a community of 350 people who built over 20 large wooden sailing ships and processed over 60,000 board feet of lumber a day.

All equipment is provided and the kayaks generally stay close to the shoreline with a guide in the lead and one at the rear.

While the Three Sisters is the destination on this tour, they are not the only interesting rock formations to be seen.

There is also a small sea cave that you get the chance to paddle into.

Kayaking around the Three Sisters at high tide is one of the most exhilarating experiences one can have, not only in Nova Scotia, but anywhere.

The Cape Chignecto area is one of unsurpassed beauty and should be explored on land and sea by every Nova Scotian. For visitors from outside the province looking for some adventure, this provincial park offers stunning views, many photo opportunities and an experience to write home about!

The approach to the cave.

WHAT YOU NEED TO KNOW:

Name: The Three Sisters, Cape Chignecto Provincial Park
Address: 1108 West Advocate Road, Advocate Harbour, NS
Websites: parks.novascotia.ca/content/cape-chignecto
driftwoodparkretreat.com
wildcaraway.com
novashores.com
Season: May to October
Time: All day
Other note: Come prepared for rugged outdoor adventures!
Classic photo op (Instagram worthy!): A classic shot of The Three Sisters

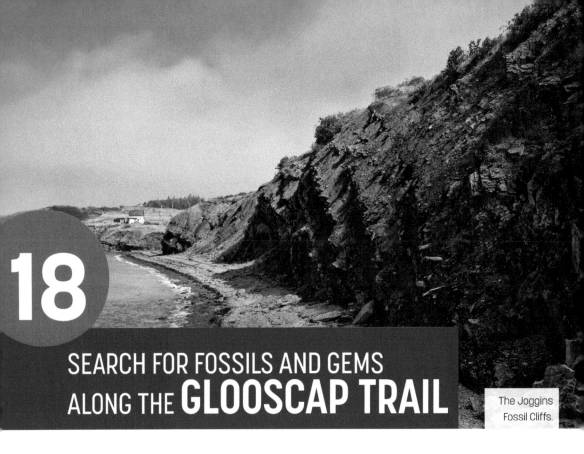

18

SEARCH FOR FOSSILS AND GEMS
ALONG THE **GLOOSCAP TRAIL**

The Joggins
Fossil Cliffs.

The Glooscap Trail is one of Nova Scotia's oldest and most scenic highways, and runs along the upper Bay of Fundy from Windsor all the way to Amherst — over 400 kilometres if you take the long version of the trail. Named for the Mi'kmaq demi-god usually referred to as Kluscap today, it contains some of the best scenery of any designated trail and is a favoured destination for archaeologists and geologists. Important fossils have been found in many places along this route. Geologists and rockhounds search the beaches and cliffs in the Parrsboro area looking for agate, the provincial gemstone, amethyst, jasper, zeolite, quartz, native copper and many other semi-precious stones and minerals.

The reason the region is such a prolific producer of fossils and collectable minerals is directly linked to the world's highest tides that flow in and out of the upper reaches of the Bay of Fundy twice a day. The tremendous amount of energy in these tides creates rapid erosion of the soft sandstones, limestones and other sedimentary rocks that make up much of the shoreline and every low tide might reveal new finds for the fossil hunter or rockhound. To get an idea of how powerful the tides are in this area, drop in to the Fundy Ocean Research Centre for Energy (FORCE), not far from Parrsboro, where tests are being conducted to find the best ways to harness this energy as renewable electricity. Many believe the future of Nova

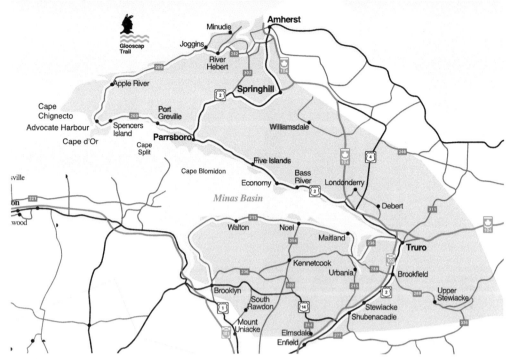

The Glooscap Trail is a scenic route that connects Windsor in Hants County with Amherst in Cumberland County.

A Carboniferous era fossil.

Scotia's ability to meet emissions standards lies in tidal power.

Although there are many places along the Glooscap Trail where fossils have been found, none is more reliable than the Joggins Fossil Cliffs, which have been designated a UNESCO World Heritage site, one of only 20 across Canada. The UNESCO website describes why Joggins received its designation:

The Joggins Fossil Cliffs, a 689 ha palaeontological site along the coast of Nova Scotia (eastern Canada), have been described as the "coal age Galápagos" due to their wealth of fossils from the Carboniferous period (354 to 290 million years ago). The rocks of this site are considered to be iconic for this period of the history of Earth and are the world's thickest and most comprehensive record of the Pennsylvanian strata (dating back 318 to 303 million years) with the most complete known fossil record of terrestrial life from that time. These include the remains and tracks of very early animals and the rainforest in which they lived, left in situ, intact and undisturbed.

In other words, there is no better place on Earth to find Carboniferous era fossils than right here in this almost forgotten part

Tetrapod tracks preserved in rock from the Joggins Fossil Cliffs.

of Cumberland County. During the late Carboniferous period, vast deposits of coal were laid down when this part of the world was a verdant wetland. Joggins was once one of the largest coal-producing areas in Nova Scotia, with evidence that the Acadians first took advantage of the coal seams as early as 1686. Active commercial mining took place for over a century, but all that ended in 1958 when the mines closed for good. The mines extended into the cliffs right up to where the cliffs ended at the shoreline. On a visit today you can see remnants of timbers high in the cliff face that were once mine shafts. The miners and local residents, who regularly walked the beaches, were continually coming across petrified trees, fossils and occasionally ancient amphibian footprints.

The town languished after the coal mines closed and, although a few visitors dropped by to look for fossils, not much was happening until 2008 when the area received its UNESCO designation and the Joggins Fossil Centre opened to the public.

Today a visit starts at the centre, where some of the best fossils found here are on display, but it's the cliffs most people come here to see. The best way to do that is on one of the three types of guided tours that are offered. These are a cursory half-hour tour, which we only recommend to someone with real time constraints, a one-and-a-half-hour tour, which is the most popular, and for the serious fossil hunters a three-hour Adventurer's Experience.

The guides are experts at identifying fossils that most people would not recognize as such. They also know where the most recent fossils have been revealed by the erosion of the cliffs. You will definitely see petrified trees, ferns and probably many other types of fossils on a guided tour. Afterwards, you are free to do your own exploring, walking in the footsteps of geological giants such as Charles Lyell, the founder of the science, and Sir William Dawson, Canada's preeminent early geologist. Thanks to the report of their discoveries to Charles Darwin, references to Joggins even appear in *On the Origin of Species*, arguably the most influential scientific treatise in history.

Finders are not keepers at Joggins and any fossils you find need to be left on site, as in all national parks and world heritage sites, to be enjoyed and studied by others.

The Joggins Fossil Cliffs are not the only place to find evidence of Nova Scotia's primordial past. The Fundy Geological Museum in Parrsboro contains a treasure trove of fossils, including the oldest dinosaur bones found in Canada and the world's smallest dinosaur footprints. For rock enthusiasts, the museum has an excellent collection of Nova Scotia gems and minerals. Getting an idea of the beautiful specimens

A stroll on the beach near Parrsboro can turn up purple amethyst (right), agate, jasper or quartz for rockhounders with a keen eye.

that can be found along the Glooscap Trail will certainly inspire some to get out and start rockhounding on their own. At the height of summer, the museum offers one-hour zodiac trips of the Parrsboro Harbour and the cliffs just outside the harbour, where both fossils and minerals are frequently found. Three times a year in late summer, the museum allows small groups to join the staff on an organized Jurassic fossil hunt.

For us, nothing beats walking along the shore at low tide almost anywhere on this coast from Economy Point to Five Islands to Parrsboro and beyond, especially at dawn or dusk. The colours on the cliffs change by the minute and you stumble across scenes with tiny waterfalls that are twice as steep as they will be at high tide.

If you can take your eyes away from what is right in front of you and look down, there is another whole world of colour and contrast to explore.

A great time to visit this area is during the annual Nova Scotia Gem and Mineral Show in Parrsboro, held in August every year since 1966. Formerly the Rockhound Roundup, it features dozens of exhibitors offering gems, minerals, jewelry and metalwork for sale as well as a variety of geological tours to some of the most interesting places on the Glooscap Trail, like Wasson's Bluff where some of the rarest fossils in the world have been found.

While driving the Cabot Trail is on every Nova Scotia bucket list (and for good reason), so the Glooscap Trail should be on your radar as well. It never fails to surprise us with its beauty, variety and splendour.

The chance to find a fossil of a creature that roamed the earth a hundred million years before the dinosaurs is reason alone!

WHAT YOU NEED TO KNOW:

Name: Joggins Fossil Cliffs
Address: 100 Main St, Joggins, NS BOL 1A0
Websites: jogginsfossilcliffs.net fundygeological.novascotia.ca fundyforce.ca
Season: April to October 9:30-5:30pm
Price: Guided tours are $10–65; children under 6 are free
Other note: Join a guided tour
Classic photo op (Instagram worthy!): A 300-million-year-old fossil

19

SAVOUR MAPLE SYRUP AT
SUGAR MOON FARM

Spile and bucket collecting maple sap.

In Nova Scotia, spring does not make a guaranteed annual appearance, where we see the days gradually get warmer, the trees start to leaf out and the birds return from their southern migration. Instead, spring tends to come in fits and starts with snow-storms often into May and temperatures not warming up consistently until June or even later. It's not our favourite time of year and we, along with thousands of other East Coasters, often head for warmer climes from March to May. That does not mean that there is nothing one can do to break the monotony of seemingly never-ending winter. Here's one suggestion that's becoming an annual rite of spring for many of us.

Most people have heard of the Blue Moon or the Blood Moon, but how many know what a Sugar Moon is and what it portends? It's the last full moon in the month of March and signals the time of year when the sap starts flowing most freely from the sugar maple trees, from which maple syrup and maple sugar are produced. A visit to Sugar Moon Farm in the Cobequid Hills during this time of year makes for a great weekend break, with the chance to do some hiking or snowshoeing, followed by a community meal in the only year-round maple sugar operation east of Quebec. Owners Quita Gray and Scott Whitelaw run a 200-acre operation that taps 2,500 sugar maple trees each spring, starting in February and running

The Rogart Mountain Trail. (Image courtesty of Cobequid Eco Trails Society.)

well into April. The maple trees are in a grove well above the main building and they are all connected by a gravity-fed system that brings the sap down to a large log building that doubles as a maple syrup production centre and a restaurant/gift shop.

Getting to Sugar Moon Farm from Halifax is a relatively easy 90-minute drive on Highway 102, making a right just past Truro onto Highway 4 at the Upper Onslow exit and then a left onto Highway 311 a short while later. Another 29 kilometres down Highway 311, there is a well-marked sign for a turn onto Alex MacDonald Road, which is gravel and can be icy in the spring. The farm is one kilometre down this road. If you get here around noon, don't be surprised if the parking lot is full and you need to park on the side of the road. At this time of year the farm is only open on Friday, Saturday and Sunday and is a very popular destination.

For first-time visitors, we recommend taking the 40-minute tour of the maple syrup operation, which costs $5 and can be booked in advance online. The tour takes place almost entirely in one small room near the entrance and is about the history of maple syrup production and how it has evolved from the Mi'kmaq through the early settlers to the modern methods that are much less labour intensive. Two wooden-carved panels show the traditional Mi'kmaq practice that produced maple sugar, but not syrup, and the earliest method of syrup production, which involved collecting the sap by hand and boiling it down in large iron vats, one of which is on display. There are quite a number of these wooden panels throughout the main building and they are all very well done.

After learning about the evolution of maple-syrup production, you conclude the tour in the unheated evaporator room, where every drop of maple syrup produced at Sugar Moon Farm is condensed from the sap collected from the 2,500 trees. Did you know that it takes 40 litres of sap to produce one

The Sugar Moon Classic with knockwurst, served with maple glazed pecans, maple whipped cream and a side of crispy bacon.

litre of maple syrup? During the tour you will also learn that sugar maples are not the only trees from which syrup can be made. There are at least ten types of maples that produce sap, as well as birch trees, many types of nut trees and even alders. Sugar maples produce by far the largest volume of sap and are the preferred choice of most maple-syrup producers. You will also learn that the taste of the finished product will vary during each season, going from almost blonde at the beginning to a very dark colour near the end. The volume of production also varies annually depending on the weather, with 2019 producing a bumper crop for Sugar Moon Farm. Finally, although Nova Scotia produces only one-half of 1 per cent of all maple syrup in North America, you will be assured that it is the best tasting — and who are we to disagree?

Before putting the maple syrup to the test, you might want to consider working up an appetite by hiking or snowshoeing the Rogart Mountain Trail that starts right at the farm parking lot. It's a 6.2-kilometre circular route that usually takes about two and a half hours to complete. It has a considerable change in elevation, so it's not suitable for cross-country skiing, but you can do that not far away at Gully Lake (see Chapter 20 for more information). This trail has four lookoffs and Jane's Waterfall to admire and photograph. If you aren't up for the entire hike, it's only one kilometre to the first lookoff, then you can return the way you came.

This trail was built and is maintained by the Cobequid Eco-Trails Society, one of the most active in the province, and now has six trails in the Cobequid Hills that all interconnect. It is part of the much more ambitious Cape to Cape trail system that eventually will connect Cape Chignecto in Cumberland County with Cape George in Antigonish County. If you have your own snowshoes bring them, but if you don't, Sugar Moon Farm has a limited number of pairs for rent. For hikers, wear waterproof, insulated hiking boots with good grips and bring hiking poles if you have them.

Another outdoor option that is not as popular as it once was since the opening of the Rogart Mountain Trail is to follow the sap line from behind the main building up through a meadow and into the sugar maples. You can use snowshoes or hiking boots for this, but there aren't any defined trails, and it can get pretty icy. Last time we were here people were body surfing on the slope.

Back at the farm, it's time for a hot meal featuring anything you can put maple syrup on. The dining room is an open area almost reminiscent of an old wooden ski lodge. Diners sit at communal picnic tables and you never know who you'll be seated with; recently it was with an Australian, a Norwegian and a Brit. Everything served here is locally produced and guaranteed fresh. Not surprisingly, pancakes, beans and bacon feature prominently, but you can also get sausages or knockwurst.

There are a wide variety of libations available, both alcoholic and non-alcoholic. This area of Nova Scotia is well known for its craft beers, ciders and distilled spirits, which Sugar Moon Farm combines in a variety of interesting ways.

For dessert, head outside and make your own from maple syrup and ice. Pour a trickle of boiling maple syrup over a bed of ice, then take a popsicle stick and roll up the syrup, which instantly hardens into a tasty treat.

Maple taffy is made by boiling maple sap just past the point where it would form maple syrup and then pouring it onto the snow.

Children absolutely love this stuff and so does Alison — a great way to end your visit to Sugar Moon Farm.

WHAT YOU NEED TO KNOW:

Name: Sugar Moon Farm
Address: 221 Alex MacDonald Rd, Tatamagouche, NS B0K 1V0
Websites: sugarmoonfarm.ca cobequidecotrails.ca
Season: Year-round; 9-4pm
Price: Trails are free to use; snowshoes available to rent
Other note: Enjoy a maple-themed lunch in the restaurant
Classic photo op (Instagram worthy!): A shot of the maple syrup as it comes out of the boiler

20

SKI THE **GULLY LAKE WILDERNESS AREA**

For those in the coastal areas of Nova Scotia who enjoy snow and the opportunity to exercise in cold temperatures, there has not been much to cheer about over the past few years. Little snow and mild temperatures have kept the cross-country skis and snowshoes in the basement much of the time. If you are prepared to drive an hour or two, there are plenty of chances and places to enjoy winter. One of those is a cross-country ski trip through the Gully Lake Wilderness Area.

In 2007 the Nova Scotia government committed to protect 12 per cent of the land mass of the province from future development by 2015. This built upon work started almost two decades earlier and has resulted in the designation of 68 wilderness areas that currently comprise close to the target of 12 per cent. These wilderness areas are chosen for the unique and irreplaceable eco-systems they represent. A report prepared in 2002 by the Department of Environment and Labour identified nine major climactic regions, 47 distinct geological formations and 84 soil types that support over 6,000 species of plants and animals and at least 20,000 invertebrates. For such a small province, that is incredible. Over the years we have visited as many of these wilderness areas as we can and no two are alike — every one of them has something amazing to recommend it.

Gully Lake was designated to protect the largest remaining hardwood stands in

A locator map showing the Gully Lake Wilderness Area.

The Gully Lake Ski Trail, in the heart of the wilderness area (bottom right).

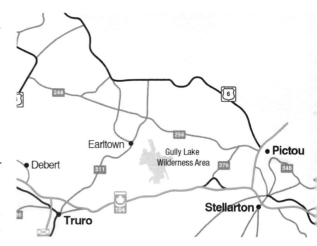

Colchester and Pictou Counties as well as the headwaters of the Salmon River, which drains into the Bay of Fundy at Truro. The area is part of the Cobequid Mountains system, which regularly receives some of the largest amounts of snowfall in mainland Nova Scotia. The higher elevations translate into snow where other areas might be getting rain. All in all, it's a pretty safe bet that Gully Lake will have plenty of snow on any given winter day.

Despite being a wilderness area, Gully Lake is quite accessible by automobile. Altogether it should take about 90 minutes from Halifax, all on paved roads. Precise directions and information on all the trails can be found at cobequidecotrails.ca. There are also coloured trail maps that can be downloaded and printed at home.

In recent years the Cobequid Eco-Trails Society has done a terrific job of establishing a series of all-season, non-motorized trails that show off the beauty of this area. Although the trailhead is shared for a short distance with a snowmobile trail, after that there are numerous choices, all of which have their own merits. It is important to know in advance that these are back-country trails that are not groomed, and they require some level of experience on skis to feel comfortable with the ups and downs of the terrain. It is a good idea to make your first visit to the area with someone who has winter experience on the trails. It may take a couple of visits before you are ready to tackle the real jewel of the system — the Gully Lake Trail.

Snowshore hare, named for its large hind feet which feet prevent it from sinking into the snow when it hops and walks.

This trail starts four kilometres from the trailhead and then completes a 10-kilometre loop that follows the course of Juniper Brook, climbing over 100 metres in elevation to cross the top of a small mountain (or large hill if you are picky) to reach Gully Lake. Along the way there are several small waterfalls, sites of old logging camps and the ominously named Small Pox clearing. Much of the trail is on old logging roads, while other parts wind through beautiful stands of birch and sugar maple, which on a sunny day cast their shadows on glistening snow that is criss-crossed with the tracks of snowshoe hare, squirrels, foxes and yes, coyotes too. The trees are festooned with many types of lichen, attesting to the clarity and healthy state of the air one breathes in here. Gully Lake is a great spot to stop for lunch, and after that it is mostly a downhill run back to the trailhead.

Other less strenuous choices include the Willard Kitchener MacDonald Trail, named for the Hermit of Gully Lake who lived in the area until his death not many years ago, and the Sandy Cope Trail named for a famed Mi'kmaq guide who travelled the area at a much earlier time.

One easy trail that follows the course of an old logging road and then a snowmobile trail leads to McIntosh Lake, which is a good place to practise your skiing form.

Another spot to reach is the oxymoronic No Name Pond.

If you ski to Gully Lake on a sunny day with little wind and good snow, you will be hooked on back-country skiing forever. We know we were.

If you don't like colder weather or feel uncomfortable on cross-country skis or snowshoes, then the time to visit Gully

Willards Falls (left) and Gully Lake Brook (right) in summer. The 25 kilometres of trails within the Gully Lake Wilderness Area pass by at least six waterfalls and provide one of the best wilderness experiences in Nova Scotia. (Images courtesty of Cobequid Eco Trails Society.)

Lake is in the late summer or early autumn when the biting insects are mostly gone, the trails are usually drier and the clean, fresh air is just as exhilarating as in winter.

The same trail system we described above is well worth hiking at this time of year and you can make Gully Lake your destination by following the old road and the now-barren snowmobile trail without having to do the entire Gully Lake Trail loop.

Another place to hike to and explore is the headwaters of the Salmon River.

Beaver dams are a common sight in this wilderness area, although you are unlikely to see a beaver as they are largely nocturnal creatures.

The Gully Lake Wilderness Area is a great place to experience some of the best of what Nova Scotia has to offer in winter and summer, and, hopefully, after visiting here you will want to see many more of these protected areas. I know we did. It sparked our interest in exploring more of our province's protected wilderness areas.

WHAT YOU NEED TO KNOW:

Name: Gully Lake Wilderness Area
Address: Kemptown Rd, Kemptown, NS
Websites: cobequidecotrails.ca
novascotia.ca/nse/protectedareas/wa_gullylake.asp
Season: Year-round
Price: Free
Other note: Be prepared and pack your wilderness essentials
Classic photo op (Instagram worthy!): Nova Scotia's scenic beauty

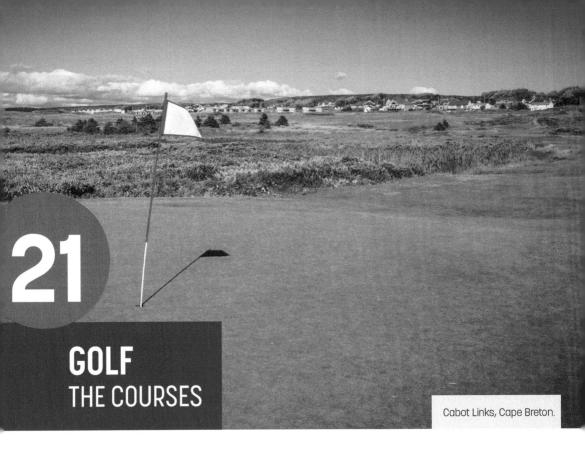

21

GOLF
THE COURSES

Cabot Links, Cape Breton.

"Golf the courses" is a line from Stompin' Tom Connors's invitation to visit his home province of Prince Edward Island by calling 800-565-7421, a number so imbued in people's memories that they can remember it decades later. While Prince Edward Island was the top destination in eastern Canada for a golf vacation when Tom first sang his song, that torch has firmly been passed to Nova Scotia. The game of golf was invented in Scotland and it should come as no surprise that it is equally popular in New Scotland. What is a surprise to many, even native Nova Scotians, is that we now have the first, fourth and eighth ranked golf courses in Canada, as chosen by SCORE Golf, the recognized arbiter of such matters in this country. Even

more surprising is that our number one course, Cabot Cliffs, is rated ninth in the entire world by *Golf Digest*. There are almost 40,000 golf courses on the planet and for Nova Scotia to have one in the top ten is an amazing feat.

Even if one has only a passing interest in this most difficult, time consuming and frustrating game described as 'A good walk spoiled' in a quote probably incorrectly attributed to Mark Twain, one owes it to oneself to play at least one round of golf at Cabot Cliffs. We promise that no matter how poorly you might play, you will remember the walk for the rest of days. For those who truly embrace the game, and plenty of Nova Scotians do, this province is a veritable treasure trove of both renowned and lesser-known courses, almost all of which feature great ocean views. We think that discovering the golf courses of Nova Scotia is a worthwhile and ultimately rewarding endeavor, regardless of what you might shoot.

It all started with Stanley Thompson, the dean of Canadian golf architects and designer of five of the top ten courses in the country. After proving his mettle at handling landscapes of great beauty and altitude changes, first at Jasper Park in 1925 and in the redesign of Banff Springs in 1928, the National Park Service (now Parks Canada) hired him to create a course of equal beauty on a fantastic piece of land that follows the course of the Clyburn Brook from its outflow into Ingonish Bay to the base of Franey Mountain in the highlands of Cape Breton. The result was Highlands Links, which Thompson considered his 'ocean and mountains' course and his best work.

For decades Highlands Links was such a phenomenal golf course that it attracted golfers from all over the world to Cape Breton to play a round on this uncompromising but undeniably beautiful layout. It went through some difficult times with federal budget cuts and unnecessary changes from Thompson's original design to make it more 'player friendly,' but a recent change in ownership of Keltic Lodge, the historic hotel associated with the course, has guaranteed its future financial viability. The course has been restored to the original design and we don't see it falling out of the Canadian top ten any time soon. Playing Highlands Links during the fall foliage season is one of the best golf experiences to be had anywhere (see kelticlodge.ca/golf/ for more information).

Playing Highlands Links during the fall foliage season, one of the best golf experiences to be had anywhere.

In 2011 Nova Scotia, as a golf destination, transcended from being very good to a must-play-once-in-your-life quest. The cause was the opening of Cabot Links on the site of an abandoned coal mine on the coast of Cape Breton, almost right in the middle of the town of Inverness. It created a sensation within the golf world. Why? It was the first true links course in Canada, and only the fifth in all North America. Of the almost 40,000 golf courses mentioned above, less than 250 are true links courses. What are the defining

The #18 green at Highland Links with Margaree Island in the distance.

characteristics of a links course? First it must abut the ocean. Second, it must essentially be one giant patch of sand on which grasses and heather might thrive, but not many trees. The best way to get the idea is to watch the British Open, which is only played on links courses. They also happen to be the oldest courses in the world. So the addition of a new club to this very special and relatively tiny family was a big deal.

As it turns out, three of the five links courses in North America are all located at Bandon Dunes in a remote area of the southern coast of Oregon. When Toronto businessman and world travelling golfer Ben Cowan-Dewar saw the sandy coastline at Inverness he knew it was a very special piece of property. He got in touch with Mike

Keiser, the man behind Bandon Dunes, and, as they say, the rest is history. The team hired Canadian golf architect Rod Whitman and after an 11-hole start in 2010, the entire 18 opened for play in 2011. On a clear and calm day (and there are many on the western shores of Cape Breton), Cabot Links is visually stunning with views of the ocean from every hole. Many links courses feature huge sand dunes that block out views of the ocean unless you climb to the top of them, but not here. The views of Margaree Island remind many of the famed Ailsa Craig off the coast of Turnberry, Scotland, a frequent host of the British Open.

The Cabot Links team did not aspire just to build a great golf course, but a great overall resort with a hotel, restaurants and club

The view from #2 tee at Cabot Links. The course offers views of the ocean from every hole.

house that fit in with the overall surroundings without overpowering them like the massive hotels associated with many of the most famous links courses, like St. Andrews. The result has been award-winning designs both inside and out.

One reason the owners went all out from the get-go at Cabot Links was that they knew they had another seafront property not far away, but completely different than the links land at Inverness. For this project, they hired the renowned design team of Bill Coore and two-time Masters champion, Ben Crenshaw. They were blown away by the amazing topography, with sheer drops from dizzying heights to crashing waves below, that is just as rare to find as true links land. This was going to be the Pebble Beach of the east, and so Cabot Cliffs was born. If Cabot Links created a sensation, Cabot Cliffs created mayhem in the golf world, with golf writers rushing to get a tee time so they could tell the world about this new course.

It rocketed up the list of the world's greatest golf courses, now sitting at ninth as of 2020.

The par-three 16th hole has rapidly become recognized as one of the great golf holes in the world, as it involves a seemingly impossible shot from one clifftop to another, with a tiny green on the other side. Conquering this hole will lead to bragging rights for life.

Other than having two of the top 100 golf courses in the world, Cabot Links (as the resort complex is called) has something else. Even though people come from around the world to play these courses (some even by a luxury cruise ship that anchors just offshore), the owners have not forgotten that this is a course in Nova Scotia and for Nova Scotians. You cannot build a resort of this calibre without charging a substantial amount for green fees, yet the prices here are very reasonable compared to courses that are much lower rated and charge more to play. For Nova Scotians and especially

The view from the #16 tee at Fox Harb'r.

junior golfers, there are reduced rates and a special Cape Breton twilight rate. This is not a place where the locals are expected to enter by the back door and know their place. They are welcomed and in fact on our last visit the starter said they were hoping to get more play from Nova Scotians, even if it meant less revenue. Visit cabotlinks.com to learn more.

A three day or more trip to Cape Breton to play Highlands Links, which incidentally is not a true links course, and the two Cabot courses should be on any golfer's wish list, but these are far from the only great courses in the province.

Another seaside course that is a pleasure to play is Fox Harb'r, the brainchild of the late Ron Joyce, co-founder of the Tim Hortons restaurant empire and originally from the small Northumberland Strait town of Tatamagouche. Designed by one of Canada's most prolific and respected golf architects, Graham Cooke, it has some of the nicest seaside holes you will find anywhere and comes in at 56 on Canada's best public

courses. Always in immaculate condition, with not a great deal of play, it's worth springing the bucks to play and stay at the resort, which has hosted Tiger Woods, Bill Clinton and other notables. Visit foxharbr. com to learn more.

Just down the road from Fox Harb'r is Northumberland Golf Links, which many Nova Scotians list as their favourite in the province. It's also got a number of seaside holes, including a famous par three with a Cape Islander fishing boat sunk in the sand at the back of the green. Green fees here are considerably less than the other courses mentioned in this chapter. Visit northumberlandlinks.com to learn more.

The Halifax area has a goodly selection of courses open to the public, including the newest: the Links at Brunello. It is a Thomas McBroom design in the suburb of Timberlea, not far from where we live, which has also arrived on the scene with a bang, holding down the 45th spot on the top 100 list. The landscape around

The Glen Arbour Golf Course.

Timberlea is not what you would readily think of as prime golf course material — the proverbial rocks and trees and more rocks and trees. Yet McBroom has pulled off some magic here by creating a very challenging test of golf that takes full advantage of the undulating terrain and the natural ponds on the property. The course has matured very quickly and is now a must-play for most local golfers. Visit thelinksatbrunello.com for more information.

Here are some other Nova Scotian courses we have played multiple times and feel confident in recommending (see the sidebar for website links):

- Glen Arbour — Another Graham Cooke design that has hosted the Women's Canadian Open and the Canadian Skins Game.
- Digby Pines — Stanley Thompson's other resort course may not be the equal of Highlands Links, but it is a good test of golf. New ownership of the Digby Pines Resort promises good things for the course and the venerable hotel and cottages.
- Chester — A municipal course on the South Shore with stunning views of the Mahone Bay islands.

While there is a lot to be said for hiking our trails, canoeing our waters, learning about our amazing history or attending festivals and special events, sometimes there's nothing like a good old game of golf, and Nova Scotia delivers that better than any place in Canada. Sorry, PEI.

USEFUL WEBSITES:
kelticlodge.ca/golf
cabotlinks.com
foxharbr.com
northumberlandlinks.com
thelinksatbrunello.com
glenarbour.com
digbypines.ca
chestergolfclub.ca

22

WATCH THE SUN SET FROM
THE SKYLINE TRAIL

The view from the Skyline Trail.

Cape Breton Island is justly famous for its amazing scenery, and perhaps no area more so than Cape Breton Highlands National Park. The park protects a great variety of ecosystems, including hardwood forested river valleys, the tundra-like highlands plateau, some of the tallest cliffs in Canada and of course the rugged coastline. While you can experience the park from behind the wheel of a motor vehicle on the legendary Cabot Trail, the best way to get to know the place is by hiking. There are 26 hiking trails that can help the adventurer experience every aspect of the park. Over the years we've been fortunate enough to hike most of them, some many times. While we can think of at least a dozen trails that would rate as world-class

hikes, none stands out in our minds more than the Skyline Trail.

We'd venture that there is no more photographed view from near the end of any trail in Canada. The combination of the Cape Breton Highlands with the Cabot Trail clinging to its side and the vast expanse of the Gulf of St. Lawrence hundreds of feet below is an unbeatable payoff for hiking the roughly four kilometres to get there.

While you certainly don't need a specific reason to hike the Skyline Trail, the one that attracts people from around the world is to watch the sunset. We're sure that, long before we evolved into the species homo sapiens, our forebears were as fascinated as we are today by the simple phenomenon of the setting

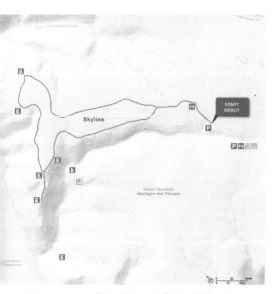

A locator map of the Skyline Trail. The full loop is a good hike during the day. For sunset watchers, there's a shorter out and back route. (Image courtesy of Cape Breton Highlands National Park.)

The panoramic views from the Skyline Trail boardwalk – you can often spot whales in the Gulf of St. Lawrence!

sun. The best sunsets are generally the ones where the sun sets directly into the water, or at least we think so.

If you look at a map of the Maritimes, it quickly becomes apparent that there are a lot more places to watch the sun rise from the sea than there are places to watch it set into the sea. The western side of Cape Breton Island is one such place, and Parks Canada has made improvements to the Skyline Trail specifically to enhance the sunset experience.

If you were hiking here during the day, it would be sensible to hike the entire 9.2-kilometre (5.7-mile) loop, but for sunset watchers, going straight in and out is the best option. To go to the very end of the trail and back is 7.5 kilometres (4.7 miles), but there are vantage points that are just as good or better well short of the end of the trail.

The Skyline Trail is probably the best maintained in the park. It is wide and a combination of gravel, earth and wooden stairs and landings, which are perfect for setting up a tripod. The walk is not taxing, but it is a gradual descent to the viewing platforms, so remember the farther down you go, the further up you must return. Remember to take a flashlight or head lamp, as you will be walking

Moose (above), bald eagles and bears frequent this habitat. Fireweed (below) can grow as tall as 5 or 6 feet.Plants are easily damaged by trampling, so hikers are asked to stay on the boardwalk.

back in less than ideal light conditions. Also, do not travel alone. This is the trail where the only known fatal coyote attack in Canada occurred in 2009. Hopefully, that was a tragic anomaly, as there have been no attacks since.

For photographers, bring a tripod or monopod. The best settings for getting the setting sun are longer exposures, which create blurs if the camera is just hand held. (We should know, 90 per cent of our sunset shots are awful!)

Our recent trip to watch the sunset was special because we did it on the summer solstice, the longest day of the year. Most of the Skyline Trail is pretty ordinary until you emerge from the forest and finally get a view of the water and the trail snaking down to the cliff's edge. By the time we arrived there were already quite a few people waiting in anticipation, as the sun seemed to grow larger and redder as Helios drove his flaming chariot closer to the horizon.

As is often the case, what appears at first

The best sunsets are when the sun sets directly into the water.

to be a totally cloudless sunset, turns out not to be. However, wispy clouds can add to the picture.

The view is breathtaking, even if there was no green flash. The green flash is a legendary phenomenon that sometimes occurs at the very moment the last of the sun disappears into the ocean. All over the world people watching the sun go down into the ocean hope to see it, but few do. Perhaps you will be lucky on your visit. Mark June 20 or 21 in your calendar each year and head to the Skyline Trail for a once-in-a-lifetime sunset. It will be the longest day of the year and the latest sunset. If it's a clear evening you just might get the best sunset photos of your life.

WHAT YOU NEED TO KNOW:

Name: The Skyline Trail
Address: On the Cabot Trail at the top of French Mountain
Websites: pc.gc.ca/en/pn-np/ns/ cbreton/activ
sunrise-sunset.org/ca/cape-breton
cbisland.com
Season: Year-round
Price: <$10
Other note: Be prepared and pack your wilderness essentials
Classic photo op (Instagram worthy!): A stunning sunset

23

TOUR THE
BIRD ISLANDS

The puffin – everyone's favourite seabird.

Dale was only about 12 years old when he was introduced to the late, great ornithologist Robie Tufts, author of the definitive *Birds of Nova Scotia*. Robie took Dale out to Evangeline Beach during the annual shorebird migration, and he was hooked for life on this most genteel of pastimes. Since preparing to write the first edition of *Exploring Nova Scotia* back in the early 1990s, we have made a point of including birding hotspots in our travels and writing.

There are almost 225 species of birds that nest in the three Maritime provinces as well as over 100 more that pass through on migrations north and south. The annual sight of hundreds of thousands of shorebirds along the Bay of Fundy in places like Shepody Bay and the Minas Basin is life affirming, and could easily be included in any Maritime bucket list. However, if one were limited to only one birding experience in Nova Scotia, we would choose a visit to the Bird Islands during the height of the seabird nesting season. The opportunity to get up close to thousands of nesting seabirds of many different species is a rare experience anywhere, yet it's quite doable just 20 minutes away from Sydney or Baddeck.

The Bird Islands, as they are usually referred to, are composed of two uninhabited islands, Hereford and Ciboux, that lie not far off Cape Breton. For many years two reputable companies have been taking birders and wildlife enthusiasts out to the islands

Bird Island Tours runs the 37-foot Cape Islander *Puffin Express*. They are Cape Breton's longest running nature tour and have been operating since 1972.

during the breeding season, which runs from June through mid-August.

Bird Island Tours (birdisland.net) runs the *Puffin Express* out of the tiny community of Big Bras d'Or. They are approximately 20 minutes west of Sydney. The way to their operation, which includes a campground and cottages, is well signed off the Trans-Canada Highway. Donelda's Puffin Boat Tours (puffinboattours.com) operates the *Highland Lass* out of Englishtown on the opposite side of Kellys Mountain, about 20 minutes east of Baddeck. Both have excellent safety records and success rates in spotting not only seabirds, but seals, dolphins and whales as well.

On our most recent trip we travelled on the *Puffin Express*, but once you are at the Bird Islands the experience will be the same regardless of which service you use.

The *Puffin Express* was purpose-built for sightseeing and can carry up to 30 passengers.

In case you've forgotten your binoculars or bird book, there are ones on board that you can share with other passengers. If you are a photographer, make sure to bring your telephoto lens and some sort of stabilizer like a unipod or bean bag — tripods are tricky on a rocking boat.

What follows is a narrative of what you might see on any given outing. Although this trip is primarily about the seabirds, there is much more to see on the way out and back.

The first thing of note is the abandoned Black Rock Point Lighthouse that is clearly deteriorating fast. When the Canadian government decided to decommission most lighthouses in Canada, the popular ones, like Peggy's Cove and Louisbourg, found societies that would look after them. Others, like Cape D'Or, found private owners who turned them into inns or restaurants. But most did not and have ended up like Black Rock Point. These buildings saved countless

Razorbills come to land only in order to breed. They nest in crevices in the cliffs or among boulders.

lives and it feels wrong to cast them aside as if their heritage is worthless.

On the other side of the channel is the bulk of Kellys Mountain, where no less than 18 bald eagles have been known to nest. Almost certainly you will see at least a few of them on any trip to the Bird Islands. There are so many eagles in the area precisely because of the existence of so much easy prey, with both the chicks and the adults of the nesting seabirds on the menu for the eagles — who have chicks of their own to raise.

The trip out to the Bird Islands offers the chance for a close-up look at the lobster fishery, which is in season in this part of Cape Breton from May 15 to July 15 — coinciding with the prime nesting period on the islands.

The waters will abound with the brightly coloured buoys marking lobster traps below and there's a good chance of seeing fishers out on their Cape Islanders hauling traps. We've never failed to be impressed by seeing this up close because, while they are using modern equipment, there is something ancient about the connection between a fisher in a small boat and the challenges of making a living from the sea.

Sightings of minke whales are also possible, but not likely as the waters here are quite shallow. However, as you near the islands you will almost certainly see hordes of seabirds in a frenzy just above the water, on the water and diving beneath the surface. They are hunting for capelin or sea smelts,

Kittiwakes nests – these birds are well known for their apparently loving nature.

Herring gulls (right) are predators, eating eggs, chicks and even adult puffins.

the small fish that are the principal diet of the nesting seabirds. Just as the eagles are here because of the seabirds, the seabirds are here because of the fish. The fish in turn are attracted by plankton that are abundant in Great Bras D'Or, the channel that connects the Bras D'Or Lakes to the open ocean. One gets a very understandable lesson on the levels of the food chain on this type of trip.

The last point of land on this part of Cape Breton Island is Cape Dauphin, which is famous for its pink granite and its legends. According to Mi'kmaq legend a cave at the end of the cape called the Fairy Hole is the home of their demigod Kluscap (Glooscap). A more modern legend, which you are very apt to hear from the captain, tells of 'the ferrymen,' a group of outlaws who posed as ordinary fishers to get close to passing boats before overwhelming and murdering the

Puffins spend most of their lives out at sea, resting on the waves when not swimming.

crews of passing ships. According to this legend the Fairy Hole hides their ill-gotten gains. We hope it is just a legend, because we find it hard to believe our Nova Scotian forebears could have been so bloodthirsty and cruel.

Not far past Cape Dauphin, Hereford, the largest of the Bird Islands, rises straight up out of the sea.

A successful seabird colony needs two things — plenty of food (i.e., the capelin and smelts), and, just as importantly, a topography that allows the birds to nest in areas that can't be reached by predators (in the case of Bird Islands, pretty well just other birds). Like humans, there are birds that can get along and nest together, like the puffins, kittiwakes, razorbills and guillemots, and ones that can't. That would be the herring and black-backed gulls. Then there are others, like the double-crested cormorants, that mess things up by just being who they are. All over North America they have destroyed countless small islands and bird colonies by their nasty habit of killing all vegetation with their deadly excrement.

As the boat approaches Hereford, named for the variety of cattle that were once pastured here, there will be more and more seabirds flying around, including guillemots, razorbills and puffins. This is certainly the time when everyone will have their cameras and binoculars out.

The puffin is everybody's favourite little seabird. With their comical looks, multi-coloured beak and friendly demeanor, they are without doubt the main attraction on the Bird Islands tour, and they nest here in abundance. The Atlantic puffin is the only puffin native to the North Atlantic, and are doing quite well on Bird Islands, if not necessarily elsewhere.

Razorbills are much easier to photograph than any of the other seabirds. They are closely related to the extinct great auk, which, as a flightless bird, was a sitting duck (pardon the bad pun) for human beings and their hangers-on like rats, cats and dogs. At one time razorbills were also endangered, but seem to have made a comeback. They are plentiful on the Bird Islands.

The kittiwake looks like a scaled-down version of the herring gull, but they are anything but in terms of their habits. Kittiwakes are not predators on their neighbours and are not scavengers. They make their living as fishing birds and are as well known for their apparently loving nature as the cry for which they are named.

The black guillemot is one of the most common birds on the islands, but it flies like a kamikaze pilot and seldom seems to sit still, making it very difficult to photograph.

There aren't many predatory birds nesting on the Bird Islands, but herring gulls and black-backed gulls top the list. They eat eggs, chicks and even adult puffins and other smaller seabirds that nest here.

We mentioned earlier that bald eagle numbers in the area are so high because of the Bird Islands. While they are usually scavengers, they will grab an easy live meal, and to them the birds on the Bird Islands provide a virtual buffet of choices. The good news is that one of their favourite snacks are gull chicks.

Seabirds are not the only attraction at the Bird Islands. Grey seals are probably right up there with the puffins in terms of what impresses most people who visit. You can't help but like them, until you realize that they eat so much fish a day that eventually it might upset this whole ecosystem.

Bird Islands is not just about the birds, mammals and fish. There are some very interesting rock formations, including the flowerpot between Hereford and Ciboux, known as the Boot.

The Boot, a sea stack (or flowerpot) created by the action of wind, rain, waves and ice on the cliffs.

Although the boats are not permitted to land on the Bird Islands, they circle both islands at close range, and there is plenty of time for photography. The trip there and back lasts about three hours and for us constitutes one of the best bargains in the Maritimes. After all, doesn't everyone have a puffin tour on their bucket list? These photogenic little birds, with their brightly coloured beaks, are the star of the show, but there's plenty more to see on this trip.

WHAT YOU NEED TO KNOW:

Name: Bird Island Boat Tours
Address: 1672 Old Route 5, Big Bras d'Or, NS
Websites: birdisland.net puffinboattours.com
Season: May to September 10 a.m.-5:30 p.m.
Price: $49 per adult and $29 per child
Other note: Dress for the weather and pack an extra sweater
Classic photo op (Instagram worthy!): A picture-perfect puffin

24

SPEND THE NIGHT IN THE
FORTRESS OF LOUISBOURG

The encampment inside
the grounds of the
Governor's Palace.

As proud Nova Scotians, we've been visiting and writing about the Fortress of Louisbourg for over 30 years. Why proud, a word we seldom use? The Fortress of Louisbourg is the largest historical recreation of a colonial settlement in all North America, larger even than Williamsburg, Virginia. To use an overused phrase that for once is entirely appropriate, it is a place that you must see to believe. Not only is the scale of the enterprise amazing, but the sheer number of re-enactors on site makes the visitor feel like they truly have stepped back in time. This was particularly true on a recent visit when Dale and a small group of friends were permitted to spend the night inside the walls of the Fortress of Louisbourg and soak up the atmosphere of this storied place.

In 1713 France ceded mainland Nova Scotia, or Acadia as it was also known, to the English after coming out on the losing side of the War of Spanish Succession. Don't ask why a war over Spain would result in the English and French duking it out in North America. The end result was that France retained Cape Breton Island, or Île Royale as they called it. They also kept their huge holdings in New France that stretched from Quebec all the way to the Gulf of Mexico via the Mississippi River. In order to protect these holdings from future English attacks, the French resolved to build an impregnable fortress at the entrance to the Gulf of St. Lawrence and thus Louisbourg, named for the recently deceased King Louis XIV, came

The massive fortress enclosed a town of 4,000 people by 1752. The one-quarter reconstruction is the largest reconstruction project in North America.

to be. It helped that the location was close to the richest fishing grounds in the world and would supply valuable dried and salted fish to Catholics in Europe who, by papal decree, were to eat fish every Friday and on other feast days.

Louisbourg was not built in a day, and in fact took decades to evolve into the massive fortress that enclosed a town of 4,000 people by 1752. It cost so much money that King Louis XV is said to have remarked that he expected to see the walls of the Fortress of Louisbourg from his palace at Versailles. There is a model on display of the completed fortress inside the restored city. By the way, it's called a fortress and not a fort because it is an enclosed fortified town, and not just a military installation. Quebec City is another example.

Despite all the money, thousands of inhabitants and a vast array of cannons, the military planners of Louisbourg forgot one little detail. They had not prepared for a land-based assault. They put all their eggs in the basket of defending an attack from the sea. The cannons all faced seaward.

The French often assumed that the English soldiers couldn't do what they ended up doing. For example, climbing the cliffs of Quebec to confront the French on the Plains of Abraham. Before General Wolfe accomplished that feat, he did something similar at Louisbourg. He landed his troops kilometres away from the fortress and trudged them and their cannons through swampy ground that the French considered impassable. Here's the kicker — it wasn't the first time the fortress had been attacked from this side! A bunch of badly trained New Englanders under William Pepperell (there's a street named after him in Halifax) did the same thing in 1745 and the fortress endured a very embarrassing surrender.

After the second fall of Louisbourg, Quebec City and Montreal followed in quick succession and at the end of the Seven Years' War, France ceded all its North American colonies, save St. Pierre and Miquelon, to England. The fortifications of Louisbourg were razed stone by stone, and by 1770 nothing was left but a massive pile of rubble with a few fisher's huts here and there.

Louisbourg remained a pile of rubble for over 150 years until Parks Canada built a museum on site in the 1930s to display artifacts. Similarly designed museums can be found at Fort Anne in Annapolis Royal and at Fort Beausejour in New Brunswick.

A few visitors are chosen each day to dress in 18th-century costumes and fire the cannons.

However, it was the decision made in 1960 that made the difference — an investment in what was essentially one of the world's largest archaeological digs at Louisbourg. Hundreds of people, many newly unemployed coal miners, were put to work rebuilding one quarter of the original town, using the same methods the French used in the 1700s. We can only say thank you to the visionaries of those times, because what they have wrought is magnificent.

The Fortress of Louisbourg experience is multi-dimensional, and for most visitors will occupy the better part of a full day. It begins outside the restored walls with a visit to a recreated fisher's hut, complete with sod roof. Here you will meet the first of dozens of appropriately costumed re-enactors who play the roles of real persons who once resided at Louisbourg.

At the fortress gates, expect to be challenged in French by a guard who is on the alert for English spies. Once you gain entry, you are free to roam the streets at will,

stopping in to any one of the many restored buildings to chat with the local inhabitants. There are two restaurants on site that serve the same food in the same manner as would have been done in 1744.

The main attraction is the Governor's Palace, which has a number of original furnishings, most of which were purchased in France to recreate the luxury afforded the king's representative in Ile Royale. The high-spired building served as the officers' barracks and through its portal are the parade grounds where troops were drilled. A select few visitors are chosen each day to dress in 18th century military costume and then, escorted by fife and drum, led to the cannons on the ramparts. Here they are permitted to fire the cannons in a ceremony that makes the tourist into a tourist attraction.

For most of its recent existence, the Fortress of Louisbourg has only been open to visitors during daylight hours. In 2015, Parks Canada started a program that allows visitors who reserve in advance several options for staying overnight. These include one of several restored buildings, the officers' barracks for larger groups or, more intriguingly, the chance to camp out inside the grounds of the Governor's Palace, using the same equipment as French soldiers would have used hundreds of years ago.

Overnight campers are supplied with a simple canvas tent, a sleeping bag, a flint kit to light a fire and a piece of beef along with root vegetables to cook up a stew. Don't expect a modern lighter. The group will eventually get their fires going, usually because someone got lucky with their flint and actually got the dried moss and bark to ignite. Once the fires are going, the pots are hung from a tripod and brought to a boil, first with just the meat and a few basic spices, like bay leaves and peppercorns, and then potatoes, carrots and turnip are added. It certainly won't be the best-tasting meal you have ever had, but it will be one the most memorable.

After darkness descends you are free to wander the now deserted town. Not surprisingly, ghosts are reputed to wander these streets and it certainly is an eerie feeling to roam through the Fortress of Louisbourg in utter quiet.

We cannot stress enough how important it is for every Nova Scotian (and visitor to the province) to visit this place, which honestly should be a UNESCO world heritage site. The experience will be greatly enhanced if you reserve in advance one of the many activities that Parks Canada is now offering.

Once you have viewed the full moon from inside the walls of the Fortress of Louisbourg or lit the fuse of a cannon while dressed in soldier's garb, you will have experienced the place as few other visitors ever have. There are many opportunities to capture unique

Dale in soldier's garb.

photographs that will transport you back in time every time you look at them. Plan ahead and make the trip to eastern Cape Breton Island — you won't be disappointed!

WHAT YOU NEED TO KNOW:
Name: Fortress Louisbourg
Address: 259 Park Service Rd, Louisbourg, NS B1C 2L2
Websites: pc.gc.ca/en/lhn-nhs/ns/louisbourg
fortressoflouisbourg.ca
Season: May to October
9:30 a.m.-5 p.m.
Price: $72 per night per tent (up to 4 people)
Other note: Stay overnight if you can!
Classic photo op (Instagram worthy!): Immserse yourself in history

25

FLY TO
SABLE ISLAND

Sable Island horses.

Choosing Sable Island as the end point for this book makes sense, because it is the ultimate Nova Scotia destination. It is by far the hardest and most expensive place to reach in the province, lying over 175 kilometres from the nearest point of mainland Canada. At the same time, it has an allure that makes those hardships petty obstacles to be overcome in the quest to see and photograph the fabled wild horses and the largest grey seal colony in the world. Birders arrive in search of the rare Ipswich sparrow, which breeds only on Sable Island. Artists are beguiled by the grasses and wildflowers billowing in the ever-present wind, by the crashing waves larger than any found on the mainland and by the patterns in the dunes made by driftwood that has floated

for perhaps thousands of kilometres. Others are fascinated by Sable's reputation as 'The Graveyard of the Atlantic' and just want to walk the beaches in search of traces of the more than 350 shipwrecks dating as far back as 1583 that occasionally reappear after being buried in the sand for centuries. In other words, there are a myriad reasons for visiting Sable Island, and thanks to its recent designation as a national park reserve, the first step to becoming a designated national park, it is much easier to get there than it has ever been.

Alison and I were fortunate enough to visit Sable Island, but on separate occasions. Alison visited on government business in her capacity as Deputy Minister of Energy, while I helped organize a small group of Explorer's

The Sable Island Trail – the closest you'll get to a road on the island!

Club members and friends, who were the first to visit Sable after it was granted national park reserve status. We both agreed that it was a day we will never forget and more than worth the trouble and expense of getting there. What follows is an account of how to get to Sable Island, what it will cost and generally what to expect when you get there.

Unlike any of the other places and experiences described in this book, even if you had the means and ability, you can't just go to Sable Island on your own. The island is administered by Parks Canada and permission and assistance from that organization is mandatory for any visitor. The starting point is to obtain the twenty-page *Guide to Sable Island National Park Reserve*, which you can find on this website: sableaviation.ca.

This useful document will provide all the information necessary to plan a visit, as well as a number of mandatory procedures to be followed in order to land on the island. The next step is to obtain a copy of the registration form from pc.sable.pc@canada.ca or 902-426-1500. The form requires identification of the people in the party, the method of getting to the island and the projected dates for a visit. The majority of visitors to Sable Island arrive by air on day trips, so once you have your Parks Canada permit you should contact the principal air service, Sable Aviation (sableaviation.ca), well in advance to determine possible dates for a visit. Sable Aviation offers only four flights a season sold at a cost of over $1,600 per seat, but these sell out very fast and only amount to 28 passengers in total. The best advice is to get your name on their waiting list for the next year's flights. Even then, nothing is guaranteed.

The better option is to organize a group of seven and charter the entire plane for a cost of around $7,500, which is less expensive than the per-seat option and offers more flexibility. Remember, Sable Aviation will not take a booking until Parks Canada has approved your visit.

Once the permission has been obtained, the booking confirmed and the weather cooperates, then the adventure begins at Halifax Stanfield International Airport,

Approaching Sable Island (above). There is no runway on the island – the plane lands on the beach. The plane journey itself is an adventure. Left is the Britten-Norman Islander that seats up to seven.

where you will board a BN-2A Britten-Norman Islander for the 300-kilometre flight to Sable Island. The plane is basically a flying tin can, extremely noisy and gets jounced around quite a bit by the North Atlantic winds. If you have any fear of flying, this is not for you, but for us it was a great part of the trip. When Sable Island first comes into view, it will send a tingle down your spine.

As the plane descends, the West Spit Light comes into view, then from a couple of hundred feet up the first horses are spotted as well as the oval-shaped lumps on the beach that are the grey seals. There is no runway on Sable Island, which might come as a bit of surprise. Instead the Parks Canada staff on the island sets out orange traffic cones on a section of the beach that they have deemed to be safe to land on. The landing is surprisingly soft, and in a matter of minutes the little plane taxis up to a couple of Parks Canada trucks. From here you are transported to an enclosed area on the island where the administration offices and staff headquarters are located and given a briefing on the 'do's and 'don't's of visiting Sable Island. The most important thing is not to walk on the dunes, but to stick to the natural paths made by the Sable Island horses. As far as the beach goes, don't get too close to the grey seals, as they can get aggressive. Once the short briefing is over, the island is yours to explore for the next eight hours or so, and with only six other visitors on an island 42-kilometres long, it's pretty much a Robinson Crusoe type experience.

Right off the bat, the Sable Island horses are the main attraction as a number of them are congregated not far from the fences that surround the administrative area. There is no consensus on how the horses (not ponies as most people call them) first came to Sable

Sable Island and the world's largest breeding colony of grey seals.

Island, but wherever and however they got there, they are now world famous. There is no need to worry about not seeing horses on Sable Island. During the days we were there they were found in quite a number of spots. The one rule with the horses was to keep your distance and not try to approach them, but still it was easy to get good photos of them.

After spending time photographing the horses, the next place to move on to is the beach on either the north or south side of the island. They are dramatically different, and you will certainly want to visit both. The beach on the south side is where you'll find the world's largest breeding colony of grey seals. Since the 1960s, the number of pups born each year has soared from just a few hundred to an estimated 50,000 births per season in recent years. Again, like the horses, you don't need to worry about not seeing the grey seals during your visit — they are everywhere along the southern part of the island. The males are surprisingly big, with an average weight of just under 300 kilograms. They have pretty formidable teeth and can

move surprisingly fast, so it's unlikely you are going to want to get that close to them.

The grey seal pups are born on Sable Island in the winter, so don't expect to see any of their cute white coats. By the time visitors arrive starting in late June, the pups have shed their white coats and now look like tiny versions of the adults.

Despite being far out in the North Atlantic, Sable Island weather is tempered by the Gulf Stream and on the days we visited in late September, it was much warmer than mainland Nova Scotia, with hundreds of seals basking in the warmth of the sun. However, you definitely would not want to consider going for a dip, as even on relatively calm days the surf is pretty wild.

Walking to the north side of the island, you come across a completely different scenario. Here is where we saw the much smaller harbour seals, along with an amazing amount of driftwood and other flotsam. The place is a beachcomber's dream, with all types of bones, shells, marine glass and plenty of items we couldn't identify, that might have

The British steamer *Skidby*, wrecked on Sable Island in 1905. The 26 crew were able to walk to shore at low tide.

been fired out of some ancient cannon. As a protected area you are only allowed to look at whatever you might find on the beaches of Sable Island and not take anything back as a souvenir of your visit.

By the time we reached the north side of the island, we were far away from any of the others in our small group and it felt like we had the island to ourselves. There was no difficulty filling the hours before the return flight by just rambling along the north beach down to the West Light and then crossing over once again to the south to walk back to

the administrative offices.

The return flight departed on time and took a bit longer than the outgoing flight because of headwinds, but far too soon for me we were back on the ground at Stanfield Airport and saying our goodbyes. It almost seemed as if it had all been a dream, so surrealistic is Sable Island in relation to any other experience we have had over our lifetimes in Nova Scotia.

It would be remiss not to mention that you can also get to Sable Island by ship, but it will cost a lot more. Up until recently two companies were including Sable Island as part of an eastern Canada itinerary, but for the near future only Adventure Canada (adventurecanada.com) is offering a once a year cruise from St. John's, Newfoundland, that will try to land on the island. Because of the unpredictable nature of the weather and the size of the surf on Sable Island, landings are not guaranteed and if they do proceed you will be sharing the island with a lot more people than you would if you come by air. Still, speaking to people who have made the landing, they recall it as a magical experience, and that sums up Sable Island: it's pure magic.

WHAT YOU NEED TO KNOW:

Name: Sable Island
Websites: pc.gc.ca/en/pn-np/ns/sable
sableaviation.ca
adventurecanada.com
Season: June to October
Price: $1500–2000
Other note: All flights are weather dependent
Classic photo op (Instagram worthy!): The Sable Island horses

INDEX